to my dear friend Mac
with christian
FROM MARC
x x

God's Good News

the book for the
new millennium

Dedication

To the memory of
W. LESLIE EMMERSON (1901-1990)
who spent his lifetime
communicating God's Good News.

ISBN 1-899505-69-5

Copyright © MILLENNIUM EDITION 2000
The Stanborough Press Ltd
All rights reserved. No part of this publication may be reproduced
in any form without prior permission from the publisher.
British Library Cataloguing in Publication Data.
A catalogue record for this book is available from the British Library.

Printed in the UK by
The Stanborough Press Ltd, Grantham

Picture credits:
Cover: Photodisc, Eyewire Images, Ron Lawrence
Pitcairn Islands Study Center – 41, 42, 43
Eric E. Ware, Avondale College Heritage Room Collection – 44
ITC – 55, 65, 101, 119, 124
Bhasker Solanki – 109, 111

God's **Good** News

David Marshall

God's Good News

Contents

God's Good News

Bible quotations are from the
NEW INTERNATIONAL VERSION
(Hodder and Stoughton, 1979)
unless indication is given to the contrary.

ABBREVIATIONS
GNB – Good News Bible, Today's English Version (Collins/Fontana, 1976)
KJV – King James Version (1611)
Moffatt – The Moffatt Translation (Hodder and Stoughton, 1964)
NASB – New American Standard Bible (A. J. Holman Company, 1973)
NEB – New English Bible (Oxford and Cambridge, 1970)
NKJV – New King James Version (Thomas Nelson, 1982)
NRSV – New Revised Standard Version (Oxford, 1989)
Phillips – J. B. Phillips, The New Testament in Modern English (Collins, 1972)
RAV – Revised Authorised Version (Samuel Bagster, 1982)
RSV – Revised Standard Version (Oxford, 1952)
The Amplified Bible (The Zondervan Corporation and the Lockman Foundation, 1987)

God's Good News

Time to Adventure

History has shifted into overdrive. Earthshaking events flash by our range of vision like a video on fast forward. Where are we going? How will it end? Does anyone know?

Societies riddled with corruption. Power in the hands of the man with the gun. Rumours of unstable dictators who have chemical, perhaps nuclear, weapons. The AIDS scourge. What does the future hold – for us, for our children?

The pace of change is unsettling. The computer revolution has proved an on-going, day-by-day struggle to keep up. Last year's state-of-the-art technology is on this year's scrap heap. Media image beamers are able to mainline into minds, to mould, reshape, according to their own agendas. But in the streets there is violence and disregard for human dignity, even human life: this is the age of fear. Planet Earth is being choked by its owners. The rainforests are being torn up, burned. Global warming; and, as holes develop in the ozone layer, the sun itself becomes a threat. Air pollution and factors yet to be identified have introduced a new range of diseases. Is there hope?

YES-S-S!

There *is* hope! Hope for today. Hope for tomorrow. Hope for you. Hope for your children.

And that hope is to be found in God's book. There we learn how to live to the full – and how to secure a hold on eternity. There we learn of God's plans for the future, of the countdown to Day Zero – and how to live through Day Zero and enter a new world, God's world. There we learn how even the biggest menaces that stalk our world – tyranny, disease, injustice – will be brought down, resolved, dissolved.

It's all in the book. Which book? The Bible.

This book is a guide to God's book. It explains why you can trust the Bible, describes God's line on the future in a fag-end world, explains God's will for every man, woman, boy and girl – and leads you to the best, the very best news there has ever been.

'The hour has come. The hour is striking, and is striking at you.'[1] No time to waste. There is danger in delay. There is an adventure to begin. Right now as you turn the page. . . .

[1]Ezekiel 7:6, 7, Moffatt.

The **Shark**
and the **Monster**

A wealthy man used to throw expensive parties on his big estate. He had an enormous swimming pool with a shark in it. At a wild, reckless party he challenged every male guest present: 'If you can dive into my pool, and swim across without the shark getting you, I will give you half of my money, half of my estate, or the hand of my beautiful daughter in marriage.'

There was a splash. A man could be seen swimming for all he was worth. With tremendous skill he evaded the shark and dragged himself out of the pool without injury. The host was amazed. He went across to the swimmer and said: 'Congratulations! I didn't think it could be done! But I'm a man of my word. Tell me, do you want half my money?'

Puffing and panting, the man said, 'No.'

'Do you want half my estate?'

Still puffing and panting, the man blurted, 'No.'

'Do you want the hand of my beautiful daughter in marriage?'

'No.'

'What *do* you want then?'

'I want you to answer just one question: *Who pushed me in?*'

In this ugly, uncertain, nervy, violent world, we may wonder, '*Who pushed me in?*'

According to legend, a monster lived outside the city of Thebes. It must have been a talking monster, because it posed a riddle to all wanting to get in or out of the city. If they couldn't answer the riddle, the monster destroyed them. The riddle: 'What has two legs, three legs, four legs; and is weakest when it has most legs?'

People were slain every day because they couldn't answer the riddle. Then Oedipus, the son of the King, answered it: 'The answer to the riddle is man. Man has two legs; but as an infant he's on all fours – that's when he's weakest; then, when he's old, he uses a stick – he's on three legs.'

And so Oedipus saved the city.

The world sets each of us a riddle. On finding an answer to that riddle depends joy, peace, a sense of purpose in this life – and eternity. Man is not the answer to this riddle. Man *is* the riddle.

The first step to solving the riddle is to answer the questions, 'Who am I?' 'What am I doing here?' 'How did I get here?' and 'Where am I going?'

Put it another way:

Who pushed me in?

This book points you

✪ to the Book of books where answers to those questions are to be found, providing you with reasons why that book is 100 per cent trustworthy;

✪ to a Man who conquered sin and death and, even now, offers you divine power to live a joyful, fulfilled, transformed life on earth – and everlasting life;

✪ to ways in which you can get to know your Creator and Redeemer on intimate terms;

✪ to the shape of your personal future, and the world's and to history's exciting climax, soon to take place.

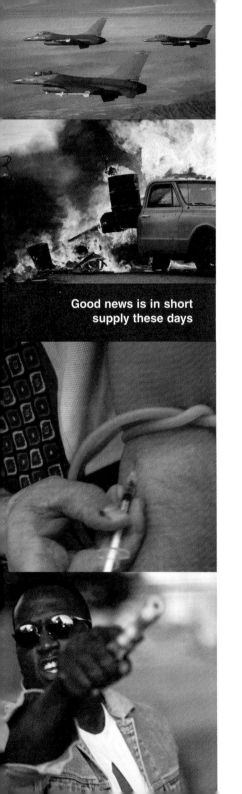

Good news is in short supply these days

Wanted!
Good News

War. Famine. Atrocity. Rape. AIDS. Earthquakes. Car crashes. Rail crashes. Plane crashes.

Violence in the streets, on the terraces, in the schools, in the home.

Organized crime. Contract killings. Old people fleeced of their savings. Muggings.

Depressing?

One BBC television newscaster thought so. 'Why can't I have some *good* news to read to the people for a change? Maybe just a single item of good news per bulletin? It's not too much to ask!'

The news editor promised to try to dig up some good news to spritz up the bulletins, but after a few weeks he gave up.

Is there any good news? You bet there is! The BBC news editor was looking in the wrong place. There *is* good news. And it comes from God, God's book – and the impact of the message of God's book on the lives of those who open themselves to it. That could, quite easily, be you. Indeed, the message of God's book is better than good news. It's the *best* news.

The message of God's book explains

why bad news overspreads the earth like foul air, *and* points to the Source of all good. It also makes sheer-clear how men and women – *bad* men and women – can be totally transformed by divine power, and discover a meaning, aim, joy, peace and satisfaction to life that, before their encounter with God and His great book, they would never have believed possible.

What's it all about?

A Nairobi workman slipped from his scaffolding and plummeted earthward. His fall was broken by the canopy on a street-side stall. Then, stunned and confused, he slipped off the canvas. He hit the pavement with a thud.

A crowd gathered. A stern policeman walked stiffly to the scene. Seeing the prostrate figure on the pavement, he asked, 'What's going on here? What's it all about?' In a daze, but beginning to recover, the workman said, 'Don't ask me! I only just arrived!'

That's how it is with us. We're comparative newcomers. We don't have a practice-run at life. We're not born with answers to such questions as 'What's it all about?' We have to discover the meaning of life for ourselves. And there are basically two alternative answers between which we have to decide:

Alternative one says, 'Life is a disease whose only cure is death. Man is just a fuss in the mud, a stir in the slime. And the human race? Its only purpose is to become fertilizer for the fields.'

Our view of the nature of man and the meaning of life is determined by what we believe about the *origins* of life and man.

Alternative One is based on the nineteenth-century Theory of Evolution. It begins with the ancestral mollusc oozing out of the primeval swamp . . . evolving over millions of years into something slightly more ambitious than a snail . . . mutating, adapting, multiplying at the expense of other species . . . until that chance arrangement of electrons and protons called Early Man took his first upright step. . . . Since then, meaningless advancement . . . towards sling and stone, sword and spear – to bullet, bomb and intercontinental ballistic missile . . . towards muggings, violence and world wars . . . towards ethnic cleansing, reigns of terror, Adolf Hitler, Idi Amin

EVOLUTION
under fire

These days, the nineteenth-century's theory of evolution is drawing heavy fire. Scientists are abandoning 'the biological faith of our time'. The London Museum of Natural History employs many scientists opposed to the Darwinian theory. They argue, 'It has so many gaps that sustaining it depends more on faith than on fact.'

Niles Eldridge of the New York Museum of Natural History says, 'The current theory is for the most part consensus, not proof.' Professor E. H. Andrews of London University has written, 'Darwinian "natural selection" is just a theory, and furthermore it is a theory riddled with the most enormous

and Pol Pot . . . towards industrial effluent, sexploitation and an over-populated planet . . . each individual, one six-billionth of the total, about as important as a grain of sand on the seashore . . . no life-purpose, no life-meaning . . . the planet itself a speck of stardust in a boundless expanse . . . birth, the gateway to a pointless pilgrimage; death, the door to final oblivion.

Alternative two is based on God's book, the Bible. The Bible insists that man was made by God, in God's image. That there *is* a purpose, a meaning, a point and a goal to it all.

Mathematicians will tell you the astronomical odds against the mollusc from the primordial swamp developing into the city slicker in the age of the computer. But the Bible does not base its message on mathematical probability but on the infinite knowledge and wisdom of the God who created, and who sustains, all things. Alternative Two insists that man is not an animal among other animals, neither a fuss in the mud, nor a stir in the slime. Man is a child of God, a child whose potential is limitless.

Alternative Two accepts God's book as the foundation of all truth; the holes. . . . It is possible to be wholly scientific and at the same time accept the opening chapters of Genesis as sober history. We need to recognize that science has its limitations. It can never ultimately account for origins.'

Many modern scientists, among them Dr David Gowart of Guy's Hospital, Professor John Walton of St Andrews University, and Dr Colin Mitchell, one of the UN's top soil scientists, have turned to biblical creationism. In their books and papers they make a convincing, scientific case for it.

The order, function, complexity, purpose and beauty in the natural world are being seen in a different light. There is that which is alien in nature, just as there is disease in man – the evidence of some evil force at work. But there is enough of design to suggest a Designer, enough of beauty to suggest an Artist, enough of scientific, structural, functional and mathematical complexity in creation to suggest an Infinite Intelligence.

personal revelation of a personal Creator who created man to be like Himself, and planned that man should live in a special relationship with God Himself. On the authority of the Bible, Alternative Two asserts that man need have no doubts as to where he came from, where he is going to, and what the whole business of life is all about.

Time plus Matter plus Chance do not make a world.

Life is not a nightmare between two eternities.

Man can find meaning in the whirlpool of life only if he acknowledges that a loving Creator God presided over Time, Life and Matter's beginning, and He will preside over Time's ending.

And that *has* to be good news.

Life *has* significance.

Your life has meaning and purpose; you are important to God; He loves you, and He has exciting plans for your life.

Alternative One is no longer obligatory.

Alternative Two is based on the Bible. So let's get into the Bible, God's book of good news.

God's **Good** News

God's book is
controversial

This book has always been a hot commodity.

People have been gaoled for reading it.

Men have been burned for translating it.

It has been banned and burned in countries scared of its influence.

During the seventy years of the Soviet Union's existence a secret network was in operation to smuggle Bibles under the 'iron curtain'. Smugglers caught distributing it disappeared without a trace. But there were hundreds of courageous men and women ready to replace them. After the fall of the Soviet Union it became apparent that God's book had kept alive the faith of millions of Christians, despite seventy years of atheistic propaganda through the media and the schools.

The first man to translate the Bible into English was hounded by the government for most of his life. After his death, his body was dug up and burned.

The next man to attempt an English translation was forced to flee the country. In Germany, as he proceeded with his task, he was shadowed by agents working for three different governments. When the project was near to completion the authorities moved in, broke up the type and came within a hair's breadth of capturing him. He escaped in a boat along the Rhine under cover of darkness. A few years later he was arrested in the Netherlands, strangled and burned.

The Bible has been ridiculed, denounced, and shot at as no other book has. The critics have attacked its factual accuracy; the characters and nations whose activities it records have been laughed off as 'mythical'. But under the fierce glare of scientific enquiry and archaeological research its

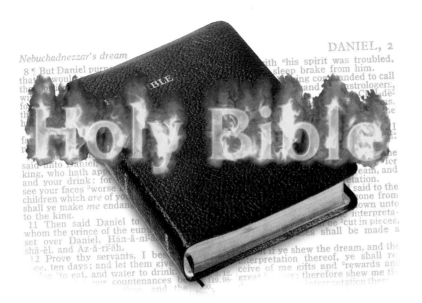

assertions have been authenticated as facts. Time and time again, its critics have withdrawn in embarrassment to regroup. The book was right. The critics were wrong.

The Bible not just relevant: essential

The world has been caricatured as one giant supermarket. In this vast supermarket everyone is a 'consumer' and every consumer is issued, at birth, with his own trolley.

The goal? By fair means or foul, to have a trolley piled higher than the next man's.

This is a metaphor for materialism.

Materialism provides no nourishment for the human spirit. It has produced *rootlessness, aimlessness, lostness, loneliness* and *disintegration*.

When the name of the game is Materialism, and the theory behind the game is Evolution, the human spirit is impoverished.

The Bible is the answer to the impoverishment of the human spirit, that aspect of man that reflects God's image, and separates man from the animals.

The Bible introduces man

✪ **To his roots.** Matter plus Time plus Chance do *not* make a world. Man, Matter and Time exist by divine command. Man was made in the image of an all-powerful, all-knowing, all-loving Creator God. He has roots among eternal things.

✪ **To his aims.** The Bible introduces man to purposeful living. The God who made man in His image loves him as an everlasting Father. Life *is* more than a dusty scuffle over a parched terrain from Point Birth to Point Death. Life *is* more than a catalogue of accidents. Life *is* more than a nightmare between two eternities. Life committed to God has purpose and aim, and both are tied up in a relationship of trust into which all comers are invited.

When God came in human flesh in the person of Jesus, He spoke of a great purpose into which each individual life may be fitted. He called – and continues to call – men and women away from humdrum lives to follow Him in a quest for a better world, a richer life, an eternal kingdom.

✪ **To life's direction.** The Bible introduces man to the Christian way, and the Christian way provides landmarks and guideposts. There is authority. Amid the babble of contradictory voices, one great voice sounds above all: the voice of God through Scripture. And Scripture provides the prophetic structure in which past, present and future are part of a whole, and that whole – our salvation.

✪ **To his fulfilment.** Materialism marginalizes and makes many lonely; the Christ of the Bible, by contrast, sought out the lonely, the woman coming to draw water, the blind man ducking and diving to avoid the crowds, the hated tax collector, the leper shunned by society, the man left at the Pool of Bethesda, the guilt-ridden Peter. And Jesus promises, 'I am with you.'

✪ **To his stability.** Materialism and human philosophy lead to disintegration. The Bible and Christianity make for stability and ultimate security. God's love is stronger than that of any parent. The God of the Bible gives no copper-bottomed guarantee that His children will not encounter problems and difficulties. What *does* He guarantee? That when the problems and difficulties come He will walk by our side and give us strength. That He hurts when we hurt. That no hurt will come our way until it has been sieved through His love, grace and power.

✪ **To fear-free living.** The God of the Bible is all-powerful. The world is more like a ship than an iceberg. The iceberg cracks off from the polar ice cap. After that, its course and destiny are subject to all kinds of uncertainties. A ship has a captain, a navigator, charts, maps, and navigational equipment. The God of the Bible is a Captain who says, 'Trust me regardless of the storms. Examine my record as set out in my Book. Trust me in the little things of time; I am concerned with the details of your life. Trust me in the big things of eternity; I want to guide you through the worst to the ultimate best.'

✪ **To guilt-free living.** God made men and women perfect. Adam gave in to the force of evil present on the planet. That force led man, with his consent, into depravity and corruption. The natural tendency of the human choice-mechanism is towards the worst, rather than the best. But the Bible tells us how, though eternal right must be maintained, eternal love found a way to save sinners through God's Son Jesus Christ.

✪ **To ultimate hope**. The Bible promises that a glorious new world – beyond the pain and injustice of the present – awaits those who enter the new life amid the sorrows and uncertainties of the *now*. In an evil-choked world, forgiveness, acceptance and high-level living are possible. In a world of conflict, it is possible to live with supernatural peace. In a world of heartbreak, it is possible to have a joy of the sort that it is in no man's power to take away from you.

God has opened the way through His Son. *Everything* is possible through trusting Him and establishing a day-by-day relationship with Him. *That* is the message of the Bible.

> **God offers a brilliant alternative to aimless despair**

The world is sick. Symptoms of the sickness are all around us. There is a cure . . .

The world is sick.

The causes of the sickness? *Rootlessness, aimlessness, lostness, loneliness* and *disintegration.*

The symptoms of the sickness? War. Violence. Greed. AIDS. The escalation of sexual offences. Pornography. The growing prevalence of diseases caused wholly or partly by stress. Divorce. Alcoholism. Drug-dependency. And much, much more.

The cure?

It is found in the Bible.

God not only inspired the thoughts behind its words; He used it to introduce Himself to us.

Through the Bible, and the God of the Bible, our horizons can be expanded. Our lives can be changed.

And this is why men have been prepared to be pilloried for reading it, burned for translating it and gaoled for expounding it.

It is the bread upon which life depends.

But what about those who lampoon the Bible, and seek to laugh off its message? What do they say? And can the Bible answer back?

The **battle**
for the Book

The Bible, strictly speaking, is not a book, but a library of sixty-six books.

Of the sixty-six books, thirty-nine make up the Old Testament. The Old Testament was written almost entirely in Hebrew.

The twenty-seven books of the New Testament were written in the Greek spoken by the ordinary man and woman: the *Koine*. The *Koine* was the international language spoken throughout the Mediterranean world in the century in which Jesus lived.

The earliest of the books of the Bible is believed to have been written before 1500BC. The most recent was completed by AD100.

The Bible was written by forty authors over that 1,600-year period.

Old Testament under attack

Controversy over the reliability and accuracy of the Bible came to a head in the eighteenth century, the Age of Reason. It particularly focused on the Old Testament.

German scholars, in particular, were adamant: The Bible had been copied out so many times down the centuries that it had 'experienced a degree of corruption beyond our wildest imagination'.

By way of answer, devout Jewish and Christian scholars could only stress that those who had copied the Scriptures over the centuries had a reputation for meticulous accuracy.

The critics said that the conservative scholars were putting too much faith in the reputation and work of those who had copied the Scriptures. No modern Bible scholars, they argued, could believe that the thirty-nine books of the Old Testament had been preserved free from error through eight centuries of copying. The biblical text had, they asserted, been corrupted. This was very much the 'establishment' view.

One day in 1947 that establishment view was unassailable.

The next day it came tumbling down.

What brought it down was a stone thrown by a young Bedouin near the Dead Sea.

Dead Sea discoveries

The young Bedouin shepherd had lobbed a stone into a hole in the wall of mountain fronting the Dead Sea. He was looking for a goat gone missing.

What he heard was the shattering of pottery.

Curiosity aroused, the youth pulled himself up to the hole, then peered into the gloom of a small cave. Soon he was running back to his Bedouin encampment as fast as his legs would carry him.

What he had seen was a number of jars with distinctively shaped caps. Did they contain gold, jewels?

On the following day, with senior members of his family, he returned to the cave. To their disappointment the jars seemed to be filled with bundles of rags. However, they felt that they might be on to something when they came across some folds of smooth brown leather.

With their finds they returned to the encampment. There, irreverent hands unrolled a scroll almost 2,000 years old. It stretched from one end of the tent to the other. They were looking at what would become known as the larger of the two Isaiah scrolls.

Market day found one of the Bedouin elders in Bethlehem. He was in earnest barter with a Syrian Christian, by trade a cobbler. The cobbler saw little practical value in the scrolls, but thought they might serve as raw materials for his shoe-mending business. For some days they were left on the floor of his cobbler's shop.

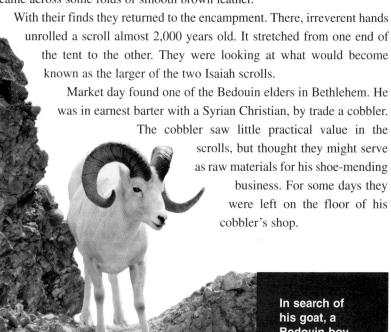

In search of his goat, a Bedouin boy discovered the first of the Dead Sea Scrolls

Then he had a bright idea. The characters on the ancient scrolls looked somehow intriguing. Up at Jerusalem there would be someone who would understand the writing and therefore the value of the scrolls.

The cobbler took the scrolls to the Syrian Convent of St Mark in the Old City. Soon expeditions were being organized to the caves. Every cave within the vicinity of the original find was being ransacked. When Jewish scholars from the Hebrew University and Christian scholars from the American School of Oriental Research became involved, they realized that they were looking at the scroll of Isaiah in pre-Christian Hebrew inscribed on papyrus.

The story was out. The original find had been made in March 1947. Twelve months later, specialists in ancient languages began to converge on the spot. There was tremendous excitement in the scholarly world. 'The Dead Sea Scrolls' made headlines all over the world.

Those questions about the accuracy of the Bible were about to be answered.

The main finds were made in caves around Qumran. Soon the caves were being numbered. One cave alone contained 35,000 scroll fragments. Eventually, ten manuscript-containing caves were found in the vicinity of Qumran.

Above, part of the Isaiah Scroll. Below, Cave 4 where it was found

Archaeologists excavating around Qumran uncovered the monastery of the Essenes. The earliest coins found on the Qumran site dated from the period 134-104BC. Central to the Qumran monastery had been the Scriptorium. Unquestionably, an important part of the work of the Essene community had been to copy out the Old Testament Scriptures, together with other literature.

It became apparent that the Essenes had fled from their monastery in AD70 when they had learned of the fall of Jerusalem. Before their flight, probably in line with a pre-arranged plan, they hid their scrolls in special jars and distributed them over a wide area in the most inaccessible caves. Whatever their expectations of their fate, it is unlikely in the extreme that the Qumran Essenes expected that their sacred Scriptures would remain undiscovered for 1,877 years.

The significance of the scrolls

Though some discoveries were still to be made, by the end of 1952 the scale of what had been found was apparent.

In modern Jerusalem is a strangely-shaped building. The visitor has to be informed that this modern building has been designed to resemble the shape of the curious caps from the jars in which the Scrolls had been found. It is called the Shrine of the Book, and has been built as a permanent home for the Scrolls, where the air is continually controlled and conditioned to make possible their indefinite preservation.

Since the discovery of the Scrolls, the central point of interest for those who converged on Jerusalem in the early 1950s was to ascertain the extent to which the 2,000-year-old Dead Sea Scrolls would uphold the accuracy of the Old Testament accepted by Christians and Jews for so long.

Thousands of hours were spent poring over photographs of the Scrolls.

By 1952 the careful comparisons were complete.

Had 'the biblical text experienced a degree of corruption beyond our wildest imagination'?

Far from it! The texts were, to all practical purposes, identical.

The text of the Old Testament had been preserved unchanged down the centuries.

The **battle** for the
New Testament

The battle for the Old Testament was won with the aid of a discovery made by a Bedouin shepherd. The battle for the New Testament was won with the aid of a discovery by a German professor.

The German professor's name: Constantin Tischendorf.

Tischendorf's studies led him to the view that the gospels *were* authored not only by eyewitnesses of the events recorded, but by Matthew, Mark, Luke and John specifically, and that the text was entirely to be trusted. While others asserted that Paul wrote only four of the New Testament letters attributed to him, Tischendorf's careful examination of language and style led him to the view that Paul had written them all.

But it frustrated Tischendorf that biblical critics were able so easily to uncover inaccuracies in vernacular New Testaments. He was angry that Bible translators had used the Greek New Testament of Erasmus (1516) so uncritically. He believed that the work of Erasmus gave rise to the inaccuracies because it was based on manuscripts that were too recent. What was needed, he decided, was an accurate Greek text of the New Testament based on the most ancient manuscripts, not on Erasmus's work. He began his search for ancient biblical manuscripts.

He examined ancient manuscripts in London, in Paris and in Rome, but found them unsatisfactory.

In 1838 he expressed the belief that, in a cobwebbed corner of some Greek or Coptic, Syrian or Armenian monastery, there were precious manuscripts slumbering in the darkness.

His search led him to St Catherine's monastery on Mount Sinai, where he discovered the largest collection of the most ancient biblical manuscripts in the world. His first visit to St Catherine's was in March 1844. In 1846 he published a brilliant edition of forty-three parchments.

But Tischendorf continued to believe that, somewhere, there was an ancient Codex of the *complete* New Testament that was older than anything found so far.

In 1853 he set off again, visiting monasteries in Libya, Cairo, Alexandria, Jerusalem, Laodicea, Smyrna and Constantinople, as well as St Catherine's on Sinai.

As the months went by, the dusty depths of St Catherine's occupied Tischendorf's imagination. He felt that there were many treasures still undiscovered.

Tischendorf undertook a third expedition to St Catherine's in 1859. At first it seemed disappointing. After several days of foraging among the dust clouds, however, Tischendorf discovered a codex which contained the whole of the Old and New Testaments in Greek. It was of incredible age.

This complete codex of the Bible became known as the *Codex Sinaiticus*. Subsequent research demonstrated to almost everyone's satisfaction that the *Codex Sinaiticus* was one of fifty accurate manuscript copies of the Bible produced between AD350-360 by a team working under Eusebius of Caesarea.

Over the centuries most monasteries in the Middle and Near East had been sacked and burned repeatedly by marauding armies. St Catherine's alone had been preserved from destruction.

Is it possible that God had had a hand in this? Indeed, that God had had a hand in preserving the Dead Sea Scrolls intact in those caves?

A page from the *Codex Sinaiticus*, a Bible handwritten before 350AD

Is it possible, too, that God enabled a German professor and a Bedouin shepherd to discover these ancient manuscripts, and thus to authenticate His Book of books at a time when it was coming under heaviest attack?

As Tischendorf studied the *Codex Sinaiticus*, the question that occupied his mind was this: Now that he had found his treasure, how would the New Testament section of this ancient manuscript compare with the text of the New Testaments then in use?

To his wife, Tischendorf wrote: 'It is the only manuscript of its type in the world. Neither the *Codex Vaticanus* (in the Vatican Library) nor the London *Alexandrinus* contains the whole New Testament, and the *Sinai Codex* is undoubtedly older than both. The discovery is a remarkable occurrence and a great one for Christian knowledge.'

Tischendorf was not exaggerating.

The professor's
discovery

St Catherine's monastery on Mount Sinai where many ancient Bible manuscripts were found

Tischendorf's final expedition had been financed by the Tsar of Russia. So he took his priceless *Codex Sinaiticus* to the Imperial Court in St Petersburg.

A codex is a manuscript in book form, as opposed to scroll form. The *Codex Sinaiticus* attracted attention throughout the world.

The Codex was to remain in St Petersburg through the Bolshevik Revolution. Financial pressures led Stalin to offer priceless manuscripts for sale. In 1933 it was bought by the British Museum for £100,000.

The significance of the Codex

In 1860 Tischendorf began working on the Codex. 'I was', he wrote, 'beside myself with joy.' The *Codex Sinaiticus* was published.

Experts accepted Tischendorf's view that the *Codex Sinaiticus* was written in the early to mid-fourth century (AD300-350). Many believed that the *Codex Vaticanus*, an incomplete Greek Bible in the Vatican Library, was of the same age.

The New Testament of the English Authorized Version (the King James Bible), published in 1611, was based, like Tyndale's version before it, on Greek manuscripts that were much more recent than the *Codex Sinaiticus*. It was, therefore, the concern of many scholars in the late nineteenth century, to compare critically the King James Bible with the *Codex Sinaiticus*.

What they found was not earth-shattering, but interesting, nevertheless.

Those who, through the centuries, copied by hand the books of the New Testament were, it would appear, guilty of a number of minor errors. In English translations of the New Testament undertaken since this time, the variations between the texts have been indicated by footnotes, for example, 'Not found in older manuscripts.'

The following represents a sample of clauses and sentences found in the King James Version that were not found in the *Codex Sinaiticus*:

✪ Mark 9:43 (second half) and 44 in the KJV present a picture of hell beloved of the hell-fire preachers of bygone centuries; 'The fire that never shall be quenched: where their worm dieth not, and the fire is not quenched.' This picture of hell is completely absent from the *Codex Sinaiticus*.

✪ The second half of Matthew 6:13 (KJV) reads: 'For thine is the kingdom, and the power, and the glory, for ever. Amen.' This is absent from the *Codex Sinaiticus*.

✪ John 4:9 (last part): 'For the Jews have no dealings with the Samaritans.' This helpful historical comment is not found in the *Codex Sinaiticus*.

The scholars believed that these minor additions/alterations had either happened accidentally or had occurred when a fragment of commentary from the margin had been incorporated into the text.

After he had spent years comparing the New Testament of the King James Version with the *Codex Sinaiticus*, British Museum curator Sir Frederic Kenyon stated: 'Our Bible, as we have it today, represents as closely as may be the actual words used by the authors of the sacred books.'

The battle continued

The battle for the New Testament had been at its fiercest in the mid-nineteenth century. F. C. Baur of the 'Tubingen School' had declared nearly all the books of the New Testament to be unauthentic. By 'unauthentic', Baur and his followers meant that the New Testament books could not have been written by either the dates or the authors assigned to them.

By discovering a handwritten Greek version of the Bible at the Sinai monastery, and by uncovering historical evidence which dated it to AD350/360, Tischendorf had put the critics on the defensive.

But he had *not* put them to rout.

'The **merest** fragment'

The critics lived to fight another day. There remained, they argued, a significant period between the first-century dates assigned to the New Testament books and the period out of which the *Codex Sinaiticus* had emerged. Christian scholars were challenged to provide 'the merest fragment' of a manuscript from between the first century, when the New Testament books were assumed to have been written, and the fourth century, in which *Sinaiticus* had been written.

This was quite a challenge!

The critics had reason to believe that the challenge could never be met. And conservative biblical scholars feared that the critics might be right.

Even the most optimistic of Christian scholars felt that 'the gap' between AD100 and AD350 would never be bridged.

But they were wrong.

Bridging 'the gap'

✪ Twin sisters, Mrs Lewis and Mrs Gibson, of Cambridge, believed that St Catherine's monastery on Sinai had yet more treasures to yield. They were right. After months of research and study, they discovered a copy of the gospels in Syriac. This copy was older than any earlier discoveries up to that time and was generally agreed to have been made around AD200.

✪ Around the turn of the century, papyrus documents preserved in the warm sands of Egypt began to be discovered. There were portions of the books of Genesis and of the Psalms which dated from the fourth century. There was a collection of the sayings of Jesus – most of which were to be found in the gospels – which dated from the third century. There was a considerable portion of the letter to the Hebrews which dated from the third century.

✪ On the banks of the Euphrates in 1920 a group of British army officers made an accidental discovery. The archaeologists were brought in. They identified what had been found as a Roman fort and, in the succeeding years, made a complete excavation of it. A synagogue and a Christian church were unearthed. Among the debris were found a number of papyri and vellum manuscripts which had been protected from the damp in a manner similar to those which had survived the centuries in the Egyptian sands. Among these was a fragment of the already discovered *Diatessaron*, which contained a mosaic of passages from all four gospels. Scholars agreed that this proved that the *Diatessaron* had existed in Greek before AD150, and that this 'commentary' on the gospels was likely to have been in circulation well before the date when the sceptics believed that the gospels themselves had been written!

✪ In 1930 the *Chester-Beatty Biblical Papyri* were discovered. The discovery was made in a coptic graveyard near the Nile. These papyri were enclosed in earthenware jars. *The Times* of 17 November 1931 reported that

Plenty of evidence

The manuscript evidence for the authenticity of the New Testament is far, far in excess of that which can be marshalled for any other document of antiquity. Over 5,300 Greek manuscripts of the New Testament, 8,000 of the Latin Vulgate and more than 9,300 manuscripts of other earlier versions are now available. This contrasts with the most authenticated work of ancient times: Homer's *Iliad*. Of Homer's *Iliad*, 643 manuscripts survive.

a large library of biblical papyri had
been discovered and that it consisted
of portions of twelve manuscripts of
which eight contained books of the
Old Testament, and three, books of the
New Testament. All agreed with Sir
Frederic Kenyon that the papyri were
'older by a century or more than the oldest manuscripts (other than very small
fragments) hitherto known'. The Chester-
Beatty collection included two substantial
manuscripts of Genesis, one from the third,

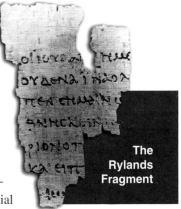

The
Rylands
Fragment

the other from the early fourth century. There were manuscripts
of Numbers and Deuteronomy – dating from the first half of the second
century! (That is, between AD100 and 150.) There were fragmentary manuscripts of Isaiah, Jeremiah, Ezekiel, Daniel and Esther dating from the late
second or early third century. The papyri of New Testament books aroused
the most interest; among them was a copy of the four gospels, plus the book
of Acts, older by a full century than the *Codex Sinaiticus*.

✪ An old fragment of John's gospel had been discovered in 1920. Now to
be found in the John Rylands University Library, Manchester, it was a torn
fragment which for centuries had helped wrap up an Egyptian mummy. It
dates from the first half of the second century AD.

The nineteenth-century critics had been unanimous in assigning the
gospel of John to a very late date indeed, and in asserting that John's authorship of it was an impossibility. The Rylands fragment of John's gospel was
proved to have been written in the first half of the second century, *in other
words, shortly after John's death (in or around AD100)*. Sir Frederic Kenyon
comments: 'Allowing even a minimum time for the circulation of the work
from its place of origin, this would throw back the date of composition so
near to the traditional date in the last decade of the first century that there is
no longer any reason to question the validity of the tradition.'

✪ The most ancient manuscript was discovered in Magdalen Library,
Oxford, where it had lain unidentified for almost a century. It was a fragment

of Matthew's gospel – *dating from before* AD70! The discovery was made on Christmas Eve 1994 by Professor Carsten Thiede.

The battle won

By 1948 Kenyon believed that the contentions of the mid nineteenth-century critics had been 'shattered to pieces'.

The time had come, he said, to reassess the value of the criticism of Scripture which had been characteristic of the previous 150 years with regard to 'the authenticity and authority of the books of which the Bible is composed'. It was time 'to shake off the excessive scepticism characteristic of much biblical scholarship in the latter part of the nineteenth century, and to restore confidence in the Bible as a guide to truth and the basis for the conduct of life'. Sir Frederic Kenyon, *The Bible and Modern Scholarship* (1948), pages 18-21.

The critics of the nineteenth century had challenged Christian scholars to provide 'the merest fragment' of a manuscript dated from between the first and the fourth centuries. In making their challenge they had been certain that 'the gap' between the time when Christians believed that the New Testament books had been completed (circa AD100) and AD350 (the date of the *Codex Sinaiticus*) would never be bridged.

They had had a veritable avalanche of fragments, plus whole libraries of papyri and even more codices. No one would challenge Kenyon's conclusion: 'A large part of the gap between the original writers and the earliest manuscripts which we possess has thus been filled.'

Against immense odds and all the probabilities, the battle for the New Testament had been won.

You *can* trust God's book of good news. The critics were in full retreat.

But the reasons for their retreat were not all connected with the discoveries of ancient manuscripts.

At the same time as the manuscripts had been discovered, the nations and cities of the Bible – laughed off as 'mythical' by the critics – had been emerging from the soils and sands of the Middle East, thanks to the spade of the archaeologist. . . .

Voices from the **ancient world**

Those who attacked the Bible not only attacked the authenticity of the text, they attacked the *accuracy* of the text. They believed that if they could prove that the historical content of the Bible was untrue or inaccurate then they would have proved that the Bible was not the Word of God.

At the dawn of the nineteenth century the argument of the 'experts' went something like this:

As history, the Old Testament was totally unreliable. Abraham and his family, had they existed at all, would have been primitives. The so-called 'laws of Moses' had nothing whatever to do with Moses. Indeed, doubt was cast on whether or not Moses would actually have been able to write! The nation of the Hittites, which loomed so large in Old Testament historical narratives, had never existed. As for the Assyrian and Babylonian kings whose names and doings peppered the Old Testament, the odd one might have existed, but most were the invention of the ever fertile Hebrew imagination. . . .

The 'experts' were guilty of bad timing as well as misinformation. No sooner had they debunked the Bible to their mutual satisfaction than the first of the three illusive keys to the ancient world was discovered.

First key: The Rosetta Stone

For centuries visitors had gazed with astonishment at the pyramids, ruined temples and long-deserted, crumbled-down cities of Egypt. They had looked in puzzlement at the story of the ancient times which had been chiselled out of stone walls and tablets thousands of years previously by Egyptian scribes. These were unread and, it was assumed, unreadable.

The Rosetta Stone

Until, that is, the discovery of the Rosetta Stone. . . .

When Napoleon invaded Egypt in 1798, he brought with him 175 scholars.

Some of Napoleon's scholars went in search of Egyptian carvings, and others in search of treasures to transport back to France. Near Rosetta on the Nile, a fascinating stone was found. Much later it was discovered to contain the record of a decree of King Ptolemy V in three languages: hieroglyphs (top); demotic script (middle); and Greek (bottom).

Napoleon's scholars had to make what arrangements they could to ship back what they had found. The ships they chartered, loaded with ancient artefacts, including the Rosetta Stone, were intercepted by the British fleet. The booty found its way to the British Museum. It is still there.

Soon both British and French scholars were studying the Rosetta Stone. Reading the Greek was easy. Once they had established that the stone contained the same decree in three different languages, they deciphered the demotic script. The hard part, however, was making sense of the hieroglyphic script.

A Frenchman made the breakthrough in 1822. Within a few months scholars were enabled to read the hieroglyphic inscriptions found all over Egypt and, by so doing, to unlock the history of a nation that cut a swathe right through the history of the Old Testament.

The ancient monuments of Egypt were covered with hieroglyphics which had remained dumb for thousands of years. Now they could speak.

The scholars – archaeologists – became aware that they were in a position to find out whether the nations and individuals whose existence was denied by the 'experts' had actually existed or not.

Second key: The Behistun Rock

Another form of writing used in most parts of the Middle East for over 3,000 years was cuneiform. Cuneiform means 'wedge-shaped'.

The use of cuneiform was commonplace for a thousand years.

In the early years of archaeological excavation, tablets containing cuneiform script were being found throughout the Middle East. It became clear that Abraham would have encountered cuneiform in Ur and, in a

The Gilgamesh Epic, a Babylonian cuneiform tablet

different form, in Egypt. It would, indeed, have accompanied him all along the trade route north-west of Syria, then south-west through Canaan. Centuries later, a man like Moses 'learned in all the wisdom of the Egyptians' would have been able to read and reproduce both hieroglyphics and cuneiform.

The story of how cuneiform was 'cracked' by scholars is tied up with the Behistun Rock.

In the spring of 1835, Henry Rawlinson, a young British army officer, was posted to Persia. Rawlinson had been fascinated by the ruins of the ancient East, and he knew that just twenty miles from base was the great Behistun Rock.

Carved high into the smoothed side of a mountain was a mysterious inscription recorded in three languages. The ancient writing had already withstood the elements of nature for over 2,000 years when Rawlinson saw it for the first time. Nobody knew what it said, or what secrets of the dim past it held.

Rawlinson decided he would decipher the inscriptions, although they covered an area of 1,200 square feet, 400 feet above the ground on the virtually inaccessible rock face. To this day, no one knows for sure how the ancients managed to smooth off the side of the mountain and write their story up there.

For fifteen years Rawlinson worked away in his spare time, in constant danger of losing life and limb, and single-handed he made careful copies of the three languages.

But it still took ten years to decipher Persian cuneiform. Then, with the assistance of experts, Susian cuneiform was deciphered. Finally, Babylonian cuneiform was identified and deciphered in 1857.

For 2,500 years the records of the ancient empires of Assyria and Babylon had been silent. They had been written in Babylonian cuneiform. Now, thanks to Rawlinson and his helpers, they could speak. . . .

Third key: Treasure tells

A tell is invariably found near a water source. In the mists of the past, a collection of families would take a decision to build a community, often in a defensible position.

With the passage of centuries their town would be destroyed by enemies. They would then rebuild on the same site (for the same reason that the settlement had been established there in the first place), building over the ruins of the first settlement.

As successive occupations would follow one upon another, a tell would gradually develop. Each occupation would be marked by its own

The Israel Stele, a tablet found in Egypt in 1896

stratum or layer. With each new settlement the area of development would decrease slightly and the town be built farther from ground level.

One way of unlocking the secret of a tell is to 'work downwards', a layer at a time. Another is the trench system by which, prior to excavation, a trench would be dug through *all* the layers of the mound.

Babylon, Nineveh, Susa, Ur, Jericho, Megiddo, Samaria and Hazor are just a few of the Bible cities which, having been silent for centuries, have yielded their secrets to the archaeologist's spade.

The door to the ancient world required three keys. The keys have been turned. The door is open. The door to the ancient world, the world of the Bible.

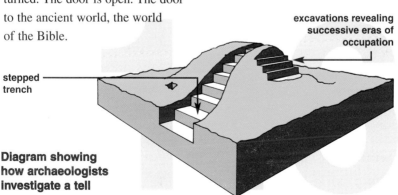

excavations revealing successive eras of occupation

stepped trench

Diagram showing how archaeologists investigate a tell

The spade confirms
the Book

The view, once held by some, that Abraham was a primitive man living in an uncivilized age has been blown away, thanks to the discoveries of twentieth-century archaeologists.

The Ur of the Chaldees excavated by Sir Leonard Woolley in the 1920s was a sophisticated city of multi-storeyed buildings with an advanced educational system. The houses of ordinary people in Ur were better built than the present-day houses of poorer people in Baghdad.

So much for primitive Abraham!

Babylon: City of gold

For 2,000 years Babylon was the key metropolis of Mesopotamia – the land between the Tigris and Euphrates rivers, now called Iraq. Famous kings like Hammurabi and Nebuchadnezzar presided over its glory days. The Greeks remembered it as containing *two* of the seven wonders of the ancient world.

At the height of Babylon's splendour, Hebrew prophet Isaiah described it

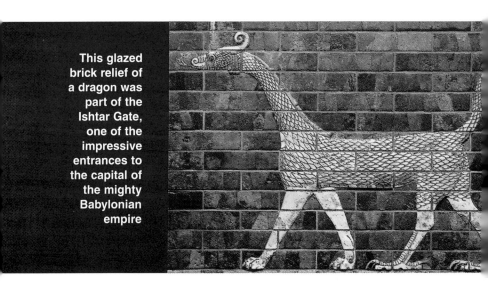

This glazed brick relief of a dragon was part of the Ishtar Gate, one of the impressive entrances to the capital of the mighty Babylonian empire

as 'the glory of kingdoms, the splendour and pride of the Chaldeans'. (Isa. 13:19, RSV.)

Archaeologist Robert Koldewey began his scientific excavation of Babylon in 1899. City walls, temples, palaces and houses were uncovered. Scores of baskets full of pottery and cartloads of stone carvings with cuneiform inscriptions were removed for study. Almost all dated from the period of Babylon's heyday, 626-539BC: *the reign of Nebuchadnezzar*. The accounts were discovered of Nebuchadnezzar's victorious campaigns against the Assyrians and Egyptians, and of his annexation of Judah. Babylonian inscriptions dovetailed with the biblical narrative.

This Babylonian cuneiform tablet records Nebuchadnezzar's defeat of Judah in 597BC

A great processional way divided ancient Babylon in half. Inscribed on paving stones and bricks was this legend: 'I am Nebuchadnezzar, King of Babylon, son of Nabopolassar, King of Babylon.' His claim reflected his boast in Scripture, 'Is not this great Babylon, which I have built . . . ?' Daniel 4:30, RSV.

Koldewey's discoveries were galling for the biblical critics. They had laughed off Nebuchadnezzar and his grandson Belshazzar as figures of myth.

The long road to Nineveh

When Sir Henry Rawlinson had completely deciphered the Behistun inscription, one of the consequences was that the site of Khorsabad, which had yielded so many inscriptions and sculptures, not to mention a vast Assyrian palace, was discovered *not* to be Nineveh. However, the palace was found to have been that of Sargon II, Sennacherib's father. Sargon, working under Shalmaneser V (see 2 Kings 18), had conquered Samaria, capital of the northern kingdom of Israel. He had left a detailed account of his conquest in cuneiform: 'I besieged and conquered Samaria and led away 27,290 inhabitants of it.'

Sargon and Shalmaneser, because previously their names had only been found in Scripture, had also been laughed off as 'mythical characters' by the sceptics.

But Khorsabad was *not* Nineveh.

Henry Layard was pursuing yet another dead-end road to Nineveh when he found Nimrud, a city built by Nimrod and known to Scripture as Calah (Gen. 10:11).

Nimrud yielded palaces, and the Black Obelisk with its reference to Hebrew King Jehu. The ivory attracted most interest. The biblical record refers to Ahab's palace 'inlaid with ivory'. (1 Kings 22:39.) The ivory in Nimrud may well have been part of the loot from Samaria.

When Nineveh was eventually found, its location was twin mounds on the opposite side of the river to present-day Mosul. There, in the Library of Ashurbanipal, were discovered tens of thousands of cuneiform documents of great historical and literary significance. Among the finds was the Gilgamesh Epic, a Babylonian version of the creation story, and the Gilgamesh Flood Epic which paralleled the Flood story in Genesis.

On the tablets in the Library of Ashurbanipal were found the names of a variety of Bible characters, including Ahab, Hezekiah, Sennacherib, Sargon and many others.

A palace, two gates and a section of wall have been excavated. But to the modern visitor Nineveh appears a wasteland. The total destruction of Assyria's cruel capital represents the fulfilment of the prophecy of Nahum.

Nahum prophesied that the capital of this Empire – which in his day stretched from the Black Sea to the northern frontiers of Ethiopia; from the sands of Arabia to the shores of the Mediterranean – would disappear without trace, and would have no mourners (Nahum 3:1-3, 5-7, 19.)

What happened to the Hittites?

At the height of the power of Syria, her army abandoned a siege and fled in terror – merely at the rumour that Israel had made an alliance with the King of the Hittites (2 Kings 7).

Part of the backdrop of the Old Testament is the powerful kingdom of the Hittites.

Nevertheless, in the eighteenth and nineteenth centuries the Hittites were a source of considerable embarrassment to both Christian and Jewish scholars. Despite the high profile of the Hittites in the Old Testament, there was no reference to such a people anywhere else. Critics insisted that the Hittites had never existed.

The excavation of the Hittite Empire began in 1876 and was undertaken by Dr A. H. Sayce. 'All of a sudden,' wrote Sayce, 'we were digging up Hittites all over the place!'

In Turkey and at Hama and Aleppo in Syria, Sayce found picture-writing on stone blocks. In 1876 he made a positive connection between these writings, the Hittites of the Old Testament and the *Kheta* named in Egyptian texts.

The Guardian of the Gate at Boghazkoy, the Hittite capital

The *Kheta* were one of the 'great powers' of the history inscribed in Egyptian stone. Before Sayce did his work, the archaeologists had been at a loss to identify them. One *Kheta* king, for example, had made a treaty with Pharaoh Ramases II. It was clear from the account of this treaty that the Pharaoh and the King had made the treaty as equals. Where could a nation be found as powerful as that of the Egyptians at the height of their supremacy?

A. H. Sayce dated the Hittite inscriptions to the centuries between 1600 and 700BC.

However, the excavation of the heartland of the Hittite Empire – in Eastern Turkey – was undertaken in the twentieth century. Between 1906 and 1912, the Hittite capital *Hattushash* – now called Boghazkoy – was excavated.

From the archives of the Hittite royal family emerged a chronology of Middle-Eastern history, and the role played by the Hittites in it during the period 1400-1200BC.

The *Encyclopaedia Britannica* devoted only eight lines to the Hittites in the 1860 edition. Today the same encyclopaedia devotes ten full pages to the Hittites.

Evidently, the Hittites were *not* one of the Bible's 'historical mistakes'.

The fact that the Bible can be trusted *is* good news. But the Bible's factual accuracy is not what makes it the Book of Good News. Those who expose themselves to the *message* of God's Good News Book find their lives being changed by miraculous means. Ever heard of the miracle on paradise island?

Miracle on paradise island

The story of the mutiny on H. [ ] 28 April 1789, was a violent one. Second-in-command Fletcher Christian, with support from twenty-five members of the *Bounty's* crew, set Captain Bligh and his nineteen loyal men adrift in a twenty-three-foot launch with 3,600 miles of open ocean between them and safety.

Christian, meanwhile, set the *Bounty* on course back to Tahiti, and the women he and other crew members had left behind there. Then, with the women on board, HMS *Bounty* set sail for an island paradise, away from the Royal Navy and their relentless search for the mutineers. Polynesian men were also taken aboard to supplement the crew of HMS *Bounty*.

Long before the lonely island hideaway of Pitcairn was spotted, the seeds of trouble had been sown. By treating the Polynesian crew members as second-class citizens, Christian had created a situation that would lead to an eruption of blood. There were constant squabbles over women.

The mutiny on HMS *Bounty* led to some amazing consequences . . .

Present-day Pitcairners are descendants of the *Bounty* mutineers

The atmosphere of demi-paradise on sub-tropical Pitcairn was to be short-lived. The amount of land capable of cultivation was strictly limited. Tension was ever present, and violence always only just beneath the surface.

With the *Bounty* burned to the water line, and no prospect of escape, the scene was set for the terror that was to provide the backdrop for the upbringing of the children of the mutineers and the Tahitian women. The death of two of the 'wives'

Plots and counter-plots. One of the Polynesian men was murdered in cold blood. One of the 'wives' poisoned a second Polynesian man. No one trusted anyone. Desperation possessed the remaining Polynesian men. They acquired firearms and set out to murder all the men against whom they had a grievance. One of the first to fall was Fletcher Christian.

In the years that followed, murder was king on Pitcairn. The women shared the guilt with the men. Within three years, only four of the men who landed on Pitcairn were still alive. Within ten years there was only one: John Adams.

Adams had enlisted on the *Bounty* under a false name, a deception made necessary by a criminal past. He was an unlikely patriarch for the strange island community that had grown up.

The *Bounty* Bible

At the close of 1800 it would have been impossible to predict what was about to happen on Pitcairn.

The island community was to be transformed.

The transformation began with a discovery.

The discovery was made by Young and Adams among the possessions of Fletcher Christian's widow.

The item discovered came to be known as 'The *Bounty* Bible'.

In his final months, mutineer Edward Young had become concerned about the future of the island. He had taught John Adams to read. The only textbook used had been the Bible, and Adams had proved an apt pupil.

After Young died of TB, Adams continued to study his textbook. He learned to read and write; but absorbed much more from God's good news book.

Soon Adams had introduced morning and evening worship services, plus two formal services at weekends.

Women and children alike noticed a change in his character and outlook. Adams had not just encountered the Book, but the Man in the Book. And that had made a drastic difference.

Adams, with Edward Young, had collaborated in a murder. Others had been responsible for the shedding of blood. They all had a past that had to

Above, the *Bounty* Bible, once the property of chief mutineer Fletcher Christian. Below, the grave of the man who used the Bible to revolutionize life on the island

be dealt with.

In the *Bounty* Bible they discovered a way to deal with the past, with sin and uncleanness. At 36, John Adams experienced a new birth.

Soon the women and children learned not only about the stories from Scripture but about the Gospel of Jesus Christ. Amazed by the change in Adams's character, they wanted to know his secret.

The new generation that had been born on Pitcairn would live to testify to the hours they h̶ ̶ ̶.̶ ̶.̶.̶nt around John Adams, ... the contents of the *Bounty* Bible. Christianity became contagious. The children caught it and practised it with enthusiasm. H. M. S. Richards says it this way: 'The children became quiet, peaceful, and hard-working. They behaved as one family, united in love under the fatherly hold of John Adams.'

The new generation on Pitcairn married in accordance with the principles of Scripture, the ceremonies being conducted by John Adams himself.

The change on Pitcairn was not short-lived.

Glyn Christian, descendant of the famous mutineer, testifies that to this day Pitcairners are Bible-believing Christians. There is no crime on Pitcairn, so there is no court, and only recently has it been necessary to appoint a part-time constable.

When visitors arrive, the strong men of the island ride the breakers in their longboats and sing of 'a land that is fairer than day'

Taste and **see**

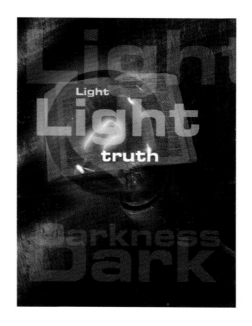

That the Bible is true is not simply because, against the longest odds imaginable, the discovery of ancient manuscripts in the last 200 years has demonstrated that its text has not been corrupted by time. Or because the findings of archaeologists have authenticated as fact the details of its narrative.

The artefacts of archaeology and manuscripts of history are merely evidences for faith. Light *is* light. Darkness is darkness. They are not what they are because of chemical tests.

Truth *is* truth.

And so the Bible is self-authenticating. The Bible is the sort of book that a man could not write if he would, and would not write if he could. The content of the Book is such that men and women, by exposing themselves to it, can discover that it is inspired by God.

The challenge is: Taste! See! Read! Discover! Adventure! And it will not be long before you find you are adventuring with God.

The Bible *is* far more than 'the world's best-seller'; *has* more, far more than 'the *ring* of truth'.

Its readers find it to be as real as the blood pulsing through their arteries, as real as the earth beneath their feet. The adventure with God into which it leads brings the reader, despite his sin-choked past, or evil-choked environment, to the chance of new birth.

Too good to be true?

There's only one way to find out.

Taste and see.

**God inspired the Bible and gave it to us because
it is a happiness recipe**

Inspired by God?

Before we read a book, we may want to know something about the author's reason for writing it.

What is he trying to say? Is he the right person to say it? Does what he says have meaning for the contemporary world?

By now we know that the Bible was written by many different authors over a period of 1,600 years. Yet despite the disparity among the forty authors – varying from kings and prime ministers to shepherds and herdsmen – and despite the long period of time that it was in the writing, the Bible has a single, unifying theme.

What about this purpose or 'unifying theme'?

Paul, who wrote much of the New Testament, set it out crisply in a letter to Timothy: 'From infancy you have known the holy scriptures, which are able to make you wise for salvation through faith in Christ Jesus. All Scripture is God-breathed and is useful for teaching, rebuking, correcting and training in righteousness, so that the man of God may be thoroughly equipped for every good work.' 2 Timothy 3:15-17.

There we have it. Origin of Book: '*God-breathed.*' Object of Book: '*Useful for human beings.*'

✪ **'God-breathed.'** Scripture, said Paul, was breathed out of the mouth of God. What was breathed out of the mouth of God the many and various writers wrote or spoke. In other words, God did not dictate the Bible. He inspired the minds of its authors, leaving them to express His inspiration in their own words.

Right off, we have one reason why the Bible was written: *It was God speaking His mind.* The Bible was a miraculous means, devised by a God of miracles in order to communicate His mind, His purposes and Himself to the children made in His image. The Bible is the Word of God through the words of men. God was speaking through men, and men were speaking from God. The Bible has a double authorship. This is what is implied by 'God-breathed'.

✪ **The Bible's usefulness.** Paul linked three words with the Bible's usefulness: '*salvation*', '*Christ*', and '*faith*'.

The first purpose of the Bible, Paul tells Timothy, is to instruct its readers about *salvation*. And salvation is a very big word. Salvation begins when a man senses his need; as long as he thinks he can manage on his own there will be no salvation. When he senses his sinfulness he will reach out to a power outside himself, and that reaching out will be sin-sorrow, or repentance.

Even before the fall of the first Adam and the entry of sin into the world, God had a contingency plan to meet the emergency. God's whole universe was built on law. Law said sin must be punished by death. And law was an expression of the character of God.

In both Old and New Testaments law is underlined. Through the words of both the prophets of the Old Testament and the apostles of the New the penalty of lawlessness, law-breaking, sin – was death.

God's central purpose in the Old Testament was to foreshadow the contingency plan to be put into practice to deal with the sin problem. It was the message of the sacrificial system in tabernacle and temple. It was the essence of the prophets' messages. It was the point of their prophecies. Sin was condemned. Sin's penalty outlined. Sin's solution prefigured, foreshadowed in a hundred different ways.

And the solution of the sin problem was in the second word Paul emphasized to Timothy: '*Christ*'. Every page of the Old Testament rustles with the rumour of a Coming One. One who would be, at the same time, 'the Mighty God' and 'the Suffering Servant'. One who, like the lambs offered on the altar, would be 'without blemish'. As the penitent confessed his sins over the head of the innocent lamb to be slaughtered, so God would send His own Lamb.

The 'Lamb of God' – in all things perfect, without blemish – would die for the sins of a fallen race. The sin problem would be resolved in the death of God's Son. Isaiah (7:14) said He would be born of a virgin. Psalm 132:11 said He would be of the house of David. Micah (5:2) said He would be born in Bethlehem. Genesis (49:10) said He would be of the tribe of Judah. Isaiah (53:3) said He would be rejected by His own people. Psalm 118:22, 23 said that this rejection would involve the rulers. Zechariah (11:12, 13) said He would be sold for thirty pieces of silver and that the money would be given to a potter. Zechariah further said that His side would be pierced (12:10), and that His disciples would forsake Him (13:7). Isaiah's fifty-third chapter had most to say about the coming One: He would suffer what men deserved to suffer; He would be silent before His accusers; He would be buried in a rich man's tomb; He would be crucified with thieves; He would pray for His persecutors. . . . The Psalmist (16:10) knew that He would rise from the dead.

These detailed predictions, made centuries before the birth of Jesus Christ, were fulfilled in His life, death and resurrection. The gospels portray Him as 'the Son of God' who, 'at the foundation of the world', had been one with the Father in love for the human race, and that the plan for the redemption of the fallen race had been entered into by both willingly.

The gospel writers presented Christ as the perfect Sacrifice for sin. Paul in his letters explained it all. Christ was the Representative or Substitute for sinful man when He died on the cross on Calvary. By identification with the dying Saviour, the penitent knew that his sins would die. And, better than that, the righteousness of Christ's perfect life would be given in exchange.

The third word used by Paul to explain why the Bible was 'useful' for human beings was *faith*.

Elsewhere Paul explained that the Scriptures were *'able to make you wise for salvation through faith in Christ Jesus'*. In short: The central purpose of the Bible is to bring us to Christ who, in turn, is the Bringer of Salvation. But the object of the Scriptures in pointing us to Christ is not simply to provide us with information about Him to enable us to understand and admire Him. The object of Scripture is to represent Jesus as absolutely worthy of our trust, to give us every reason to place implicit faith in Him and in His sacrifice for sin.

That unpromising candidate for salvation, John Adams, grasped all this from his reading of the *Bounty* Bible. The result? His life was transformed, and, through his influence, so were the lives of the other islanders.

Down through the ages, *millions* – yes, *millions* – testify to that experience.

Every happy-ending story begins with the Bible. The Bible exposes the reader to Jesus Christ, its central Figure. Through Jesus, the Man in the Book, come both faith and salvation.

Can we afford to wait another minute before we encounter this Jesus?

God's Good News

Meet Jesus

The main source of information about Jesus is in the four gospels. They were written by men who knew Jesus personally. They are the most obvious sources of information about Him.

A good place to start reading the Bible is with the gospel of Mark. It is believed that Mark wrote from Peter's dictation, and Peter was one of the foremost followers of Jesus. How fascinating to find that it is in Mark's gospel that Peter appears in the worst light! One of Mark's stories implies that, in addition to setting down Peter's recollections of Jesus, he knew Jesus at first hand.

There are many details in the four gospel accounts that would have been left out of modern biographies. John the Baptist, at one point, is described as having his doubts regarding the credentials of Jesus; 'Are you the One who was to come, or should we expect someone else?' Like a good reporter, the apostle John records the negative audience-reaction to the sermon recorded in John 6 (verses 41-43, 52, 60, 61). Jesus' loss of a mass following is candidly recorded (John 6:66). Matthew records that in His home town Jesus did not work many miracles (Matt. 13:58). Luke reports the words of unbelievers who regarded Christianity as a superstition (Acts 25:18, 19).

All the gospel writers report the initial disbelief of the disciples about the news of the resurrection. Peter had left the tomb 'wondering to himself what had happened'. The others 'did not understand from Scripture that Jesus had to rise from the dead'. 'They did not believe the women (who first brought the news of the resurrection), because their words seemed to them like nonsense.' Even after the final appearance of Jesus 'some doubted'. Eventually Jesus Himself had 'rebuked them for their lack of faith and their stubborn refusal to believe'. (Luke 24:11, 12; John 20:9; Matt. 28:17; Mark 16:14.)

In a letter written to Christians in Corinth, before the first gospel was committed to paper, Paul lists those who saw Jesus alive after His very public death. Concluding the list, he said that 'over 500 Christians' saw Jesus after the resurrection, 'of whom', he says, 'the majority are still alive' and hence available for interview. (1 Cor. 15, Phillips.)

Short of embellishing the reputation of Jesus, again and again the gospel writers provide us with examples that show that accurate reportage was more important to them than making a good impression.

The gospel writers set out bluntly the claims of Jesus to be the Christ, the Messiah, God's Son. Jesus is the only man who ever lived who claimed to be God yet was judged sane by his wisest contemporaries. Confucius did not claim to be God; neither did Zoroaster, nor Buddha, nor Muhammad. They had too much regard for their credibility. C. S. Lewis was correct with regard to the claims of Jesus. He said that, given such claims, Jesus had to be mad or bad – or God. No one, apparently, is suggesting that He was mad or bad. True enough, some have made the claim that He was 'simply a great teacher'. But how could He have been – making such claims? He did not leave us that option. He was mad, or bad – or God.

An unlikely hero

Jesus emerges from the gospel accounts an unpromising hero. He was born in an outhouse, not a palace. He was brought up in a bad locality: men doubted if any*thing* – and, by implication, any*one* – good could come out of it. There are no records of His having received a formal education, though He learned much at His mother's knee, in His father's workshop, and at the synagogue. He was a practical man and, when He left home, lived rough out of doors. He had a capacity to inspire loyalty, but only among *ordinary* men. He knew few of 'the right people'.

He avoided the limelight and refused political position. He never entered what we would call a big city and never went over the frontiers of His own small country.

The plot of the Jesus story is hardly the stuff of a hero's tale. His first three decades were unexceptional: only His mother cherished dreams of greater things. After He left the home place, He made some impact as an itinerant preacher-cum-healer. But there was no rise and rise to fame and fortune. To those who would 'win friends and influence people' His career was a saga of missed opportunities. His words of wisdom very often were either not understood or misunderstood. He quite simply did not have the knack of saying the 'right' things. In the end, all but a nucleus of His followers 'walked no more with Him'.

Then there was His end: aged 33, still in His prime. Betrayed by a friend. Arrested. A sham trial under cover of darkness. Voices formerly used to cheer Him on demanded His execution. A contrived sentence. Death between two gangsters.

Finis. The end.

The really remarkable thing about His story was that the end was only the beginning.

Three days following His execution, a persistent rumour ran through the crowded streets and bazaars of bank-holiday Jerusalem that He had risen from the tomb. Not long after that, His small group of followers, so recently cowering and browbeaten, now radiating inextinguishable hope and unshakeable confidence, were preaching His resurrection from the dead. All this to the anger of those who had conspired in the corridors of power to bring Him to execution. What they wouldn't have done to destroy and discredit those converting thousands in a day to the cause of the risen Christ! But the only thing they needed to do to prick the bubble was to walk a distance no greater than two hundred yards beyond Jerusalem's walls; that is, if the tomb was *not* empty. . . .

The tomb of Jesus Christ *was* empty. Friends and enemies knew it. The fact was beyond dispute. So no one disputed it.

The **good news** of the **cross**

In the years ahead, the cause of the good news about Jesus Christ was unstoppable. Of course, there were those who *tried* to stop it – by fire, stoning, and, indeed, any means available. But one of the foremost detractors, Saul of Tarsus, became the foremost exponent of Christ's cause and the foremost preacher of the good news.

'I, if I be lifted up from the earth,' Jesus had said, 'will draw all men unto me.' He *had* been lifted up – on a cross, the most hideous instrument of execution which the evil imagination of man had devised to date – and men *were* drawn to Him. Thousands of them. For upon that cross hung the Good News for all ages.

When most of that original group of followers had met violent deaths preaching the good news, another generation emerged to lift up Jesus – and men and women continued to be drawn. Through the age of furious persecution associated with emperors like Nero and Diocletian, men were drawn into the cause of the Nazarene.

When Christianity grew to 'respectability', it melded with heathenism, became rotten, and, for a time, the good news was lost sight of. But there were still pure spirits that kept it alive, and did so in the catacombs under great cities and in the caves of the mountains. Despite the worst that persecuting powers could do, men were still drawn by the magnetism of Jesus.

When the lines between truth and error were drawn in the sharp, clear light of the Reformation, men like Luther, Zwingli and Calvin drew thousands by preaching the good news. In England some were burned alive at Smithfield and Oxford for their convictions regarding the good news about Jesus Christ. But the cause of Christ and the good news prospered.

In the Age of Reason, when Christianity had again compromised with prevailing social attitudes, John Wesley travelled 6,000 miles a year on horseback lifting up Jesus and His Gospel – preaching out of doors chiefly, under the same cathedral dome where Jesus had done His own preaching – and the history of a nation was redirected.

Since Wesley, there have been many others – George Whitfield, D. L. Moody, C. H. Spurgeon, Billy Graham, James Aggrey, H. M. S. Richards – the list is endless. The message and the effect, the same: the good news of salvation.

In *our* postmodern age, world-wide, millions claim to be followers of the unpromising hero from the unlikely background. Asked to summarize the good news about Jesus Christ, Christians choose His words in the night-time interview with Nicodemus. Many have said that this is the greatest verse in the Book:

'For God so loved the world, that he gave his only begotten Son, that whosoever believeth in him should not perish, but have everlasting life.' John 3:16, KJV.

Why is it the greatest verse? Because it concerns the greatest Giver: God. It alludes to the greatest thing in the world: love. It refers to the greatest group it is possible to love: the world. It mentions the greatest evidence of love: giving. It enshrines the greatest gift ever bestowed: the only begotten Son of God. It includes the greatest invitation: whosoever. It is the greatest text because the only condition mentioned is of the greatest simplicity: believing. Because it concerns avoiding the greatest fate: perishing. Because it promises the greatest reward: everlasting life.

The gift was made on Calvary. On the tick of prophecy and in the destined place and context of events, need, personnel and circumstances, the Son had come to earth to give His life for the salvation of the human race.

So if Calvary was so important, what *really* happened there?

What really happened at **Calvary**?

Before the body of an assassination victim is cold, long before the debris from a plane crash has been collected together, and before the survivors have been cut free in a train smash – people want to know WHY? Public investigations are called for.

Many decades after the death of John F. Kennedy, some are still investigating his assassination; millions are dissatisfied with the explanations given thus far and conspiracy theories are rife. Many questions are still outstanding about the death of Diana, Princess of Wales.

But have you ever really investigated the death of Jesus of Nazareth? Surely His was the most mysterious death of all time. What was the inside story?

It happened on 14 Nisan, a Friday, AD31, outside Jerusalem. But what brought it about? Was it an accident? Was it planned? If so, by whom? Why did He die? Was His death the greatest tragedy in the history of the planet?

What were the events that led up to it?

Countdown to Calvary

The cross had long been casting its chill shadow over the sun-warmed landscape of Judaea as, on the preceding Sunday, thirteen men passed under the Golden Gate of Jerusalem. Jesus and His disciples had come south for the Feast of the Passover, AD31, in the reign of Tiberius Caesar.

Only in the eyes of Jesus was there the glint of apprehension that the boisterous adulation of the chanting pilgrims would, in days, turn into the frenzied howling of a turbulent rabble thirsting for blood.

Jesus knew of the tangled skein of passions, prejudices and intrigues already being woven by His enemies. He had challenged and healed His way from one end of Israel's *status quo* to the other. With the swish of a sentence He had exposed mistaken, dangerous beliefs. Sightless eyes had been made to see. The ears of the deaf had been unstopped. The daylight of reason had been let into shuttered minds. The sorrowing and downtrodden had rediscovered laughter. Sinners had been received and transformed. The power of death had been defied. Lazarus, dead for four days, was alive again and, as everyone knew, was living, working and enjoying life within walking distance of Jerusalem.

For these things the political bosses, the chief priests and scribes, could not forgive Jesus. His very existence was a reproof to them. His presence in Jerusalem was their opportunity to do Him to death.

They did not know that they were moving to the rhythm of prophecy.

Jesus had come to the Feast of the Passover to be Himself the Passover Lamb; 'the Lamb of God that taketh away the sin of the world'. He had come to offer Himself as a sacrifice: not for one man or a select few, a Chosen

Jesus died on the cross – not as a victim or a martyr – but to make possible our salvation

People, but as a ransom for all mankind, always.

The sacrifice Jesus had come to make was to enable man to give himself to God, washed clean of sin by the blood of this (human-divine) Passover Lamb, reborn into a new life, covered with the righteousness of Him who was about to die the death the sinner deserved so that the sinner might have everlasting life.

The glory of the cross

The shouting of Palm Sunday soon subsided. As Jesus stood with His disciples in the Temple not long after, a very different atmosphere prevailed. Rejection had to be faced. The voices which cried 'Hosanna' would soon be hoarse with a much more sinister chant.

It was at this time that a message was brought to Jesus from a group of Greeks visiting Jerusalem. The investigation had begun – *before* His death. Hearing conflicting rumours, they had come to find out the truth for themselves. They found a disciple and said: ' "Sir . . . we would like to see Jesus." ' John 12:21.

To Jesus, this was significant. These foreigners represented the great multitude from the Gentile world who would be drawn into the good news when He had been 'lifted up'.

Nevertheless, His words were surprising: ' *"The hour has come for the Son of Man to be glorified."* ' Verse 23.

✪ Not much glory in Gethsemane, the place of betrayal and arrest. Sweat-drops of blood as He pressed His face to the cold, hard ground. The awful feeling of separation from His Father as He bore the collective weight of all the world's wickedness. The agony of betrayal by a friend for thirty pieces of silver.

✪ Not much glory before Annas, Caiaphas, Herod and Pilate, the Roman governor. Cruel sham trials under cover of darkness. The mockery, the scourging, and the purple robe. As the first grey preliminaries of dawn began to appear on that infamous Friday, the vast, drummed-up multitude of those He had healed and helped, those who days before had cried 'Hosanna', now cried 'Crucify'.

✪ The curious confrontation with Pilate: the sophisticated Roman and the

Galilean; the man of the world and the man not of this world; Caesar's representative in Judaea, and God on earth.

✪ Condemnation and the thorn crown. Jesus dragging the cross along the Way of Sorrows to the Place of Skulls; a man stumbling along, bearing on His back the frame onto which He would be stretched and nailed.

✪ Not much glory on Calvary. Nails through His wrists and feet. Hoisted aloft in searing agony. Shifting His weight from arms to legs and back again: pain beyond endurance. His tongue stuck to the roof of His mouth. Death of a broken heart at the ninth hour. Lightning slashing through the sky in angry stabs. The earth shaking. And, above it all, His voice crying, *'It is finished.'*

What really happened?

' *"The hour has come for the Son of Man to be glorified."* '

But in the days that followed the entry into Jerusalem of those thirteen men – where was the glory?

Gethsemane

Jesus existed before earth-history began; present at the creation of a perfect planet (John 1:1-5). Before earth and time began, evil had originated in heaven – in the breast of heaven's chief chorister, Lucifer. There had been war in heaven. Lucifer, or Satan, and a third of the heavenly host who had fought with him on the side of evil had been expelled from heaven (Rev. 12:7-9; Isa. 14:12-14). Jesus had witnessed the expulsion. In the hearing of seventy-two followers He said, ' "I saw Satan fall like lightning from heaven." ' Luke 10:18. In the newly-created earth, Satan had conned the first man and the first woman with his primal lies: ' "You will not surely die" ' and ' "You will be like God" ' (Gen. 3:4, 5).

After the sin of the first man, the chain of sin had remained unbroken. Satan's purpose: to lead the whole world astray (Rev. 12:9). Satan had become man's great accuser before God; since all had sinned, he demanded that all should be damned (Rev. 12:10-12; Rom. 3:23). Jesus had come to earth to break the chain of sin, uninterrupted since Adam, and set the people free. He had been born to live a perfect life and, by dying a blameless death, to enable the sinner to receive salvation. From the first, Satan's agents on earth, from Herod to Pilate, had sought to destroy God's Son. In Gethsemane and on Calvary they thought they had triumphed.

With the creation of earth, the war in heaven had been transferred to the surface of this planet. The decisive battle in that war occurred in Gethsemane.

Jesus and His disciples had left the upper room. Judas, thinking violently, had long since descended into the darkness and had scurried away to join the high-born conspirators. Jesus and the eleven made their way through the city gates and across the brook Kidron. He became strangely silent. He had spent many nights in prayer to His Father. But there had never been a night like this one. The awful burden of the world's guilt weighed heavily upon Him. By actual experience He was beginning to taste death for everyone. A titanic struggle raged in His soul. Clinging to the hard, cold ground, He said: 'Oh my Father, if it is possible, let this cup pass . . . .'

Then the most important word in the Book: ' . . . *nevertheless*.' The salvation of the human race hung on a word. The enemy of God must succeed now or be for ever doomed. Nothing was inevitable about what happened in Gethsemane. It had all been *prophesied*, but not *predetermined*. Would Jesus wipe the blood sweat from His brow and leave humanity to perish in its own cesspit of sin? Or would He bridge the river of sin and death for everyone?

But the words *were* said. The decision *was* made.

'*Nevertheless* not as I will, but as You will.'

When the priests and scribes and the temple guard, their blazing torches almost engulfed by the thunderous blackness of that darkest-of-all midnights, and Judas, ready to plant his kiss, entered the olive garden, the battle was over. The victory had been won. The nails *would* be hammered. The spear *would* be thrust. Fallen humanity – and that's you and me – would find its salvation.

So there was glory in Gethsemane. *It was the glory of victory.*

Before Pilate

But how was there glory before Pilate? Pilate asked, 'What shall I do with Jesus?' – a question we all must answer.

The rabble cried, 'Crucify', and Christ was condemned. He bore it all in

Many people in the crowd still choose to turn their backs on God

silence. 'I find no fault in Him', said Pilate. But Pilate was first a politician. Caesar's man. As Judas had thrown down his thirty pieces of silver at the feet of the conspirators, Pilate tried to wash his hands of the guilt of shedding innocent blood. But Judas found that the kiss was not so easily disposed of as the silver; the kiss would last for ever. For Pilate, no water could wash away the stain and curse which he carried to his grave.

But how little did any of the players but one know what was taking place! How little did they understand *who* was on trial! They thought they had placed Jesus on trial before Pilate. But only a few short hours before, they themselves, each one of them, had as it were, stood on trial before Jesus in the Garden; and He, knowing what they would do, knowing what they would shout, had held to His decision to save them.

Yes; there was glory, even before Pilate. It was a glory that was serene and confident: *the glory of the knowledge of triumph.*

The Place of Skulls

Wherein was the glory of the cross?

Agony and death; hideous, writhing, obscene. A vast crowd, cat-calling. Voices hissing with aggression. Upturned faces, many grotesque with hatred and scorn. *Recognizable* faces. Weeping faces.

Some of the faces have a curious modern look about them. Were *you* there when they crucified my Lord? I was. My face was in the crowd. For, apart from the *visible* crowd, there was the invisible multitude of all who had ever lived, and would ever live until the ending of the world.

A cacophony of derisive voices tauntingly cried, 'Save yourself – if you can!' Jesus cried, 'Father, forgive them; for they know not what they do.'

Why did **Jesus** have to **die**?

Only Jesus, the perfect Son of God, could pay the price of sin. God's broken law was as changeless as His character. The penalty for that broken law was death. Jesus, wholly man and wholly God, paid the penalty. He died as *our* substitute, in *our* place.

Paying the price

Jesus, the sinless one, bore the sins of all the world so that, when we accept Him as our personal Saviour, we might receive the gift of His perfect righteousness and be saved (2 Cor. 5:21).

Repeat these words, and read the Bible texts that come after them, and you will begin to understand the meaning of the cross:

The condemnation was Thine that the justification might be mine. The agony was Thine that the victory might be mine. The pain was Thine that the healing might be mine. The curse was Thine, that the blessing might be mine. The crown of thorns was Thine, that the crown of glory might be mine. The death was Thine,

Jesus died to set us free; His sacrifice is the key to our salvation

that the life purchased might be mine. (2 Cor. 5:21. Rom. 4:24, 25. 1 Cor. 15:3. Gal. 1:4. Eph. 1:7, 8. Eph. 5:2. Rom. 3:25. 1 John 2:2; 4:10. 1 Peter 1:18, 19.)

One voice

As soon as Jesus was spread-eagled upon the wood and began to bleed, He said, 'Father, forgive them'. As soon as the blood flowed, He was interceding with His Father. And His intercession is a clue to our *fundamental* problem and our *fundamental* need. Our fundamental problem, basic to all others, is sin. Our fundamental need, basic to all others, is forgiveness. Forgiveness is the bridge over which all must pass who would enter God's kingdom.

Dark clouds hung over the three crosses; two gangsters had been crucified, their crosses jolted into place on either side of the suffering Jesus. The mob speculated as to what foul omen was represented by the thick, almost touchable, darkness. The rabble failed to realize that Jesus had entered the outer darkness of separation from God – *and all for them.*

Above the shrieking and howling – 'Save yourself! If you can!' – one solitary voice, near the Saviour's ear, said, 'Save *me!*'

Only one man understood what was happening on the Place of Skulls – and he was a thief. For centuries the people of Israel had brought lambs without blemish to the temple to be slain as a pointer to the Lamb of God who would one day come and die to atone for the sins of the world. Beyond the searing agony and indignity of it all, only a thief recognized in the man on the next cross the Passover Lamb, God's only begotten Son.

What will *you* do?

Shall we howl with the frenzied rabble, you and I, or shall we echo the words of the penitent thief?

Jesus was dying for the evil that men have done, said and thought; and dying the cruellest death ever devised, to provide mankind for ever with a fount of joy and hope, an inspiration to high endeavour and an assurance of salvation.

John, who led the heartbroken mother of Jesus from the awful scene, lived into old age. But, in exile for his beliefs, his hair white, his hands unsteady, John could not forget the thrill of what he had seen and heard and handled of the Word of Life (1 John 1:1). He wanted to set down on paper what, through the inspiration of the Spirit, he remembered so vividly – before it was too late. As he took up his quill pen, for a moment he was carried away. He found himself again looking on the three crosses on that dreadful Friday. And he wrote: *'And we beheld his glory . . . as of the only begotten of the Father,' 'He came unto his own, and his own received him not. But as many as received him, to them gave he power to become the sons of God, even to them that believed on his name.'* John 1:14, 11, 12, KJV.

Jesus died with a shout of triumph – He had accomplished our salvation

The glory of the cross was the glory of a finished redemption for as many as received Him. The key to the meaning of it all was in the words of Jesus that sounded over the confusion of men's voices: *'It is finished.'*

The atonement for sin was accomplished.

The price of sin had been paid. The chain of sin, uninterrupted since Adam, had been broken.

Through the years of my life, the days of my years and the hours of my days, I shall hear Him saying, 'Father, forgive them,' and I shall know He means me.

I know, too, that He means *you*. What is it to you? What will *you* do with Jesus?

Risen indeed!

Three pm Black Friday. 'It is finished,' they heard Him cry; and then He died.

By sunset, when the Sabbath hours began, His lifeless body had been buried in Joseph's new tomb.

The empty cross on the green hill looked like a symbol of failure. Whatever mission He had sought to accomplish – it appeared to have misfired.

As late as the following Sunday afternoon, walking to Emmaus, one of His disciples said to his two companions: ' "We had hoped that he was the one who was going to redeem Israel." ' Luke 24:21. Notice *'had hoped'*; now hope had gone. Because of the speaker's tears he had not realized that the third member of the party, who had just joined them, was the risen Christ Himself.

What with Roman guards and Roman seals and mighty stones, Jesus had been locked in His rock prison as securely as if He were to remain there till the end of time.

But before the sun had risen that first Sunday morning, the news was spreading that Jesus Christ was risen! That the grave had given up its victory and that the living Son of the living God, a dead man an hour ago, had in the lonely morning been seen and spoken to!

The women were the first to see Him. Then Peter and John, off at a fast gallop, discovered that the greatest event of human history had broken about their ears.

Gradually the good news sank in. The cry, 'It is finished', had been a shout of triumph.

It is accomplished. *What* is accomplished? All barriers between man and God had been removed. God could do no more: that is why the cross is judgement – refused, it is the end of hope. Christ need do no more; that is why the cross redeems. Accepted, it is the end of all endeavour to save ourselves.

Now that Jesus of Nazareth had walked out of the tomb with the tread of a conqueror, the events of the preceding days looked very different.

Calvary, like Gethsemane, had been a battlefield. The decisive showdown between, on the one hand, good and God and, on the other, the devil and evil had taken place. The great controversy, begun in heaven, had been decided on earth. Now it is approaching its conclusion.

The first Christians believed that Jesus rose because they saw Him alive again, and the acid test of the resurrection is still personal encounter.

The fact and power of the resurrection launched what G. K. Chesterton called 'a winged thunderbolt of everlasting enthusiasm'. From Jerusalem, an intensely heated centre of burning zeal, a vast field of lava was thrown out to the limits of the Roman world. But the men at the centre of all this had fled from Gethsemane! One had denied his Lord with oaths! All had spent the period between crucifixion and resurrection holed up behind bolted doors.

Suddenly, the very same men were preaching the resurrection before vast crowds, converting thousands. What made the difference? A personal encounter with the risen Lord, and the power of His Holy Spirit.

Paul encountered the risen Christ on his way to wipe out Christianity in Damascus. His resistance crumbled on the instant of the encounter. And this Paul – fearless, educated and fired up by the Spirit – was to do more than any of Christ's champions to explain the meaning of His life, death and resurrection.

Paul was to travel thousands of miles by foot, horse and ship to spread the good news of the Gospel to the Roman world. And this man of action, always on the move, found time to commit to paper the letters that made clear the good news of the Gospel to every generation, including ours.

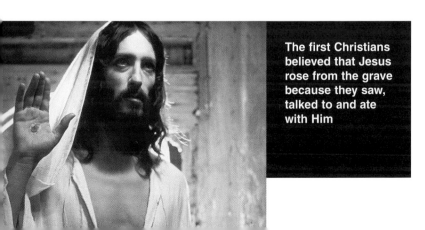

The first Christians believed that Jesus rose from the grave because they saw, talked to and ate with Him

A come-as-you-are **party!**

Charlotte Elliott was a carefree cockney who lived at the time when the Revolution began in France. She became popular by writing satirical verses and drawing satirical cartoons.

Her carefree life ended when, at 30, she began to suffer from a degenerative disease. For the next fifty years she was more-or-less bedridden. When the disease struck, she sank into deep depression. Her humour and gift for satire left her. Death seemed close. Pastors were called in, but what they said increased the deep sense of guilt she already had. She felt she could not come to Jesus for salvation because she was not good enough.

Then Dr Malan, a new pastor, came to visit. He homed in on her problem: 'You are right to feel a sense of sin; the apostle Paul says that "all have sinned". Without a sense of sin no one comes to the Saviour for pardon and new life. But if you wait until you are good enough to come to Jesus, you will wait for ever. You must come as you are, a sinner, to the Lamb of God

Sin has made our world a place of uncertainty and unhappiness

that taketh away the sin of the world.'

Charlotte came to the Saviour. Just as she was.

And that is the only way anyone can come to Jesus. We cannot be 'good enough' to deserve salvation. We come to Jesus in sin-sorrow (repentance) with hand outstretched – the *empty* hand of faith.

A broken law

Jesus died for the sins of the world; because the law of God had been broken. The law of God defines sin. In the first letter he wrote to the early Christians, Paul said, 'The law was our schoolmaster to bring us unto Christ, that we might be justified by faith.' Galatians 3:24, KJV. The law makes us aware of our sin, of our need of a Saviour, that we cannot *deserve* salvation.

Modern theologians argue that 'the law has been done away with'. But to reject Jesus Christ at Sinai is to reject Him at the cross. Jesus is both Creator and Redeemer (John 1:1, 3, 10; Eph. 3:9; Heb. 1:1, 2). Jesus was on Sinai and at Calvary – one and the same, ever one God. The God of Sinai was at Calvary because the law He had given man on Sinai was as changeless as His character, for it was an expression of it, and because that changeless law had been broken. Sin had challenged God's law and, because that law must stand or the universe must fall, because the law represents the foundation principles of right which cannot be set aside, the Son of God came to accept man's blame and die man's death – on Calvary.

'The wages of sin is death.' Romans 6:23. 'Sin is the transgression of the law.' 1 John 3:4, KJV. God's love for man, as changeless as His law, made Him send His only Son to die because of man's transgression. He did this that man might have the choice of eternal life, as opposed to the eternal death that would otherwise have been his lot (John 3:16).

God's stone-written record of ten eternal principles of right was considered 'holy, and just, and good' by Paul (Rom. 7:12, KJV), 'the law of liberty' by James (James 2:12, KJV), and claimed as His own by Jesus who said, 'If you love me, keep *my* commandments' (John 14:15, KJV).

In Jesus' great Sermon on the Mount, far from doing away with the law, He said that it was not enough that our actions should be right; our thoughts and motives should be pure (Matt. 5:26-28). He began His teaching with the words: ' "Do not think that I have come to abolish the law . . ." ' (verse 17).

Paul grasped the teaching of Jesus. 'No one will be declared righteous in his sight by observing the law; rather, through the law we become conscious of sin.' Romans 3:20. The law is there to cut down our self-righteousness, to show us our true condition. The law is a mirror. But the law cannot change us any more than a mirror can change our physical features.

So what is the 'condition' of man before he comes to Jesus?

Luther described unregenerate man as 'crookedly bent in on himself'. He must come to Jesus crooked. Only the Lord can straighten him out.

'I did it my way'?

There is no do-it-yourself salvation. Salvation is a gift that you can have only if, in repentance, you go to the Saviour and accept it. But without sin-sorrow there is no sense of need. If there is no sense of need, we shall not be drawn to the cross. No cross, no Saviour, no salvation, no crown – no conversion.

Paul begins the third chapter of his letter to the Christians in Rome by proving that 'whoever we are' we 'are all under sin'. 'What shall we conclude then? Are we any better? Not at all!' Romans 3:9. 'For all have sinned . . . .' Verse 23. We all start from the same touchline: a long way from righteousness.

**Salvation comes as a gift.
You cannot earn it**

There is only one way to come to Jesus: as a penitent. 'For it is by grace you have been saved, through faith – and this not from yourselves, it is the gift of God – not by works, so that no one can boast.' Ephesians 2:8, 9. When sin-sorrow brings us to Jesus, we have that all-important personal encounter. We reach out and accept Jesus as our Saviour, our Substitute. We are then 'justified' before God; by His great grace we are credited with the righteous character of the One who died for us.

The *guilt* of sin is taken away when we are justified. As we grow into Christ, the Holy Spirit is the agent through whom the *power* of sin diminishes in our experience. But there is never any scope for boasting. The nearer we come to Christ the more aware we become of the reservoir of evil within us. Hence the really great Christians are the ones most acutely aware of their propensity for sin.

Years after his dramatic conversion, 'Amazing Grace' author John Newton wrote: 'I am not what I *ought* to be! Ah! how imperfect and deficient! I am not what I *wish* to be! I abhor that which is evil, and I would cleave to that which is good! I am not what I *hope* to be! Soon, soon, I shall put off mortality, and with mortality all sin and imperfection! Yet, though I am not what I ought to be, nor what I wish to be, nor what I hope to be, I can truly say I am not what I once was, a slave to sin and Satan, and I can heartily join with the apostle and acknowledge, "By the grace of God, I am what I am!" '

How Jesus saves

That's how it is with all of us. In Romans 3:21-24, Paul contrasts the reservoir of evil within man with what he calls 'a righteousness from God' or 'a righteousness of God'. This *other* kind of righteousness – the only *genuine* kind – is, says Paul, 'apart from the law'. Martin Luther's whole life was totally transformed when he stopped being intimidated by the phrase 'the righteousness of God' and realized that this righteousness is a free gift which the believing soul receives from God through faith in Jesus Christ.

As Romans 3 concludes, Paul is telling us that as we cast our burden of guilt at the foot of the cross, we must leave there, too, all our deadly doing – all our attempts to achieve salvation by performance. 'Did this make the law null and void? Not at all!' Law-keeping was the fruit, not the root, of our salvation.

Remember Charlotte Elliott? Bedridden for fifty years? Remember the words of Dr Malan, 'You must come as you are, a sinner, to the Lamb of God that taketh away the sin of the world'? Those words led to Charlotte's conversion. Through the remainder of her bedridden life, she celebrated each day with a renewal of her personal relationship with Jesus. She considered every day a new spiritual birthday.

Eventually, Charlotte began to write again; not satirical verses, but another kind of verse. Fourteen years after her conversion, having thought about the words of Dr Malan many times, she incorporated them into the words of a hymn that every sinner should read as he makes his way to the Saviour:

Just as I am – without one plea,
But that Thy blood was shed for me,
And that Thou bidst me come to Thee,
O Lamb of God, I come. I come.
– *Charlotte Elliott (1789-1871).*

Living life
right in the **fast lane**

When we come to Jesus, we come as we are. It is the only way. We cannot make ourselves good.

But we do not *stay* as we are.

That is why Jesus said to His night-time visitor, Nicodemus, 'No one can see the kingdom of God unless he is born again.' John 3:3. The complete U-turn demanded by Jesus of all who would travel in the fast lane with God, shocked this member of the Jewish ruling council. Jesus then explained that the radical life-change was only possible by a miracle that would take place when the sinner co-operated with the Spirit of God. And this miracle would be occasioned when he had seen Jesus 'lifted up' (John 3:1-15).

Beneath the cross of Jesus

When we, with hymn-writer Isaac Watts, 'survey the wondrous cross on which the Prince of Glory died', we realize that the love response called for is 'my soul, my life, my all'.

Paul explained this revolutionary experience in the Christian's life in terms used in the law courts.

When we come to Jesus in sin-sorrow (repentance) and ask for forgiveness, we are 'justified'. Justified is the opposite of 'condemned' but means more than forgiveness. By God's free grace and the faith (trust) He gives us, we are justified or declared righteous. Justification involves both a *subtraction* and an *addition*. Our sins are subtracted. The righteousness of our Saviour is added. God treats us as if we had never sinned (Rom. 3:21-26; 4:1-3; 5:1, 2; Eph. 2:4-9).

So justification is much more than acquittal. It is a new start to a new life. The guilt of sin has been removed; the U-turn made; and we start in a new direction by the Spirit's power.

When Paul had just finished explaining justification, however, he wrote, 'Do we, then, nullify the law . . . ? Not at all! Rather, we uphold the law.' Romans 3:31. 'For we are God's workmanship, created in Christ Jesus to do good works, which God prepared in advance for us to do.' Ephesians 2:10.

Relationship, not rules

Paul wanted the Christian to understand that his life was one of total dependence *on* God; and took the form of a day-by-day relationship *with* God. In this relationship there would be a growth in spiritual maturity. Part of this growth would be that sin would lose its grip on the Christian; its power would wane in his life. God's 'new creation' (Gal. 6:15) would not 'conform' to the world's way but would be 'transformed' (Rom. 12:2).

The first thought of every transformed Christian is to follow God's revealed will – including His law – in all things. The Christian does this, not in order to be saved, but because he is saved. Thus keeping God's commandments is the fruit (natural result) of the Christian's salvation. Jesus told His disciples that those who constantly 'abide in the Vine' (Himself) will experience the sap of the Spirit in their lives, and 'bear much fruit, showing yourselves to be my disciples' (John 15:1-8).

Accidents on the road

Of course, on God's fast track the Christian may have accidents, even reversals. But there is always a Saviour willing to forgive and renew (1 John 1:9). Justification is not a once-in-a-lifetime experience. It is a daily experience. But, despite the war with waning sin, those whose lives are 'in Christ Jesus' need fear 'no condemnation' (Rom. 7:14-8:1). The Christian pronounced justified cannot then sin with impunity, nor will he want to do so. The *burden* of sin has been removed and for those 'in Christ' the *power* of sin will diminish. The Christian will experience the assurance of God's salvation (Romans 5:1, 2).

Paul was especially concerned to stress the relationship of the Christian with the Risen Christ. He wanted the Christian to know that this is not a knife-edge, on-off relationship, but that Christ can in all things be trusted:

'If God is for us, who can be against us? He who did not spare his own Son, but gave him up for us all – how will he not also, along with him, graciously give us all things? Who will bring any charge against those whom God has chosen? It is God who justifies. Who is he that condemns? Christ Jesus, who died – more than that, who was raised to life – is at the right hand of God and is also interceding for us. Who shall separate us from the love of

God wants **spiritual fruit**, NOT **religious nuts** . . .

On His way to the Garden of Gethsemane on the night of His betrayal, Jesus led His disciples through a vineyard. In the upper room, where they had celebrated the Last Supper, He had explained to them that when He had gone away the Holy Spirit would come. In the vineyard he explained part of the work of the Holy Spirit.

' "I am the true vine and my Father is the gardener," ' said Jesus. ' "He cuts off every branch in me that bears no fruit, while every branch that does bear fruit he prunes so that it will be even more fruitful." ' John 15:1, 2. Jesus went on to explain that as the life-giving sap of the Spirit flowed from the roots through the vine stock to the branches (us), then the branches would bear 'fruit', 'more fruit', and 'much fruit'. ' "This is my Father's glory, that you bear much fruit, showing yourselves to be my disciples," ' Jesus concluded (verse 8).

There was one great point of emphasis in what Jesus said. Bearing fruit was a natural process; a consequence of the indwelling Spirit. Without that indwelling Spirit there could be no fruit at all (verse 5). With the Holy Spirit there could be an abundance of fruit and this abundance would bring real joy to us, and to our Heavenly Father (verse 11).

Paul put it like this: 'Live by the Spirit, and you will not gratify the desires of the sinful nature.' Galatians 5:16.

The Christian way is an upward way to glory. Those who, after an outburst of temper, say: 'That's just how I am! Take it or leave it!' are not Christians. The Holy Spirit is there to change how we are.

And how does that change take place? After conversion we co-operate with Him in the work He seeks to do in our lives. Paul details it this way: 'The fruit of the Spirit is love, joy, peace, patience, kindness, goodness, faithfulness, gentleness and self-control.' Galatians 5:22, 23.

It is during hardship that it becomes evident whether we have or have not the Holy Spirit and the life-fruits the Holy Spirit brings. As we bear the fruit of the Spirit in our lives, others will see in us 'the family likeness of his Son'. (Rom. 8:29, Phillips.)

Christ? Shall trouble or hardship or persecution or famine or nakedness or danger or sword? . . . No, in all these things we are more than conquerors through Him who loved us. For I am convinced that neither death nor life, neither angels nor demons, neither the present nor the future, nor any powers, neither height nor depth, nor anything else in all creation, will be able to separate us from the love of God that is in Christ Jesus our Lord.' Romans 8:31-39.

The fast-track life – with Jesus

Do Christians ever experience discouragement? Yes; when they concentrate their minds on the sin, instead of on the Saviour. A great Christian once wrote: 'In the way that leads to the city of God there are no difficulties that those who trust in Him may not overcome. There are no dangers which they may not escape. There is not a sorrow, not a grievance, not a human weakness for which He has not provided a remedy. In our conflict with evil we have a mighty Champion who has never lost a battle.'

At the new birth when we accept Jesus, we are thrown into the heart of the battle. Beforehand, we had merely been on the edge. Then the arrows fly thick and fast. But there is good news. We have a panoply above us, and a shield before us, that will resist the fiery darts of the wicked one.

Martin Luther wrote: 'If at any stage we look at ourselves we wonder how we could ever be saved. But if at any stage we look at Him we wonder how we could ever be lost.'

Christians do get discouraged – often when they *feel* they are on their own in the battle against sin

God in sharp focus

The Bible is rather like my camera. It does not have automatic focus. The subject of the Bible is the character of God. God is in sharper focus in some parts of Scripture than He is in others. If you look for God's character in some of the history recorded in the Book of Judges the picture will be, to say the least, very blurred. Look for it in Isaiah (say in chapter 53) or in Hosea, and suddenly it is so much sharper. But look for it in the gospels, in Jesus, and it's as sharp as it can be. Jesus is the only complete, sharp-focus picture of God.

Jesus told His disciples: ' "Anyone who has seen me has seen the Father. . . . I am in the Father, and the Father is in me." ' John 14:9-11. Jesus is God in sharp focus. And in God there is no unchristlikeness at all. If there's something in the Old Testament that appears to conflict with Christ's character, it's because there's something we have not understood.

There are two places – at least – in the gospels where God's character shines through so sharply that my eyes water, and there is a lump in my throat. One is at Calvary. The other is in three stories that Jesus told to illustrate a key characteristic of His Father.

A revolutionary picture of God

The chapter begins with Pharisees grumbling about Jesus: ' "This man welcomes sinners, and eats with them," ' they said (Luke 15:1, 2).

These Pharisees were the respectable people of the day and were very good at calling other people 'sinners'. They had a saying, 'There is joy in heaven over one sinner who is destroyed before God.' Jesus knew this and deliberately presented the opposite picture of His Father: 'There is joy in heaven over one sinner who repents.'

✪ **The lost sheep.** The first of the three stories concerns a shepherd with a hundred sheep, one of which got lost. He left ninety-nine in the fold and, over hazardous terrain, went in search of the lost sheep until he found it. Then the shepherd returned to his village with the lost sheep across his shoulders. The whole community turned out to help him celebrate. There was a great shout of joy and a feast of thanksgiving. Jesus said, ' "I say to you that likewise there will be more joy in heaven over one sinner who repents than over ninety-nine just persons who need no repentance." ' (Verse 7, RAV.) Heaven throws a party whenever one lost, solitary earthling chooses to return to the warmth and light of the Father's presence. And the Father (God) cheers the loudest!

○ **The lost coin.** The second story concerns a woman who lost one of the coins on her headband. This was no ordinary coin; it symbolized the fact that she was a married woman. Jewish homes had dirt floors covered by straw that was not changed very often. The picture is of the woman scrambling around among the dirty straw, a candle in one hand, until the coin was found. Here is a picture of how God, in Jesus, came from the glories of heaven to search for you and for me in the filth of earth. When the woman found the coin she called her neighbours in for a celebration. When God found you, and found me, there was a special celebration in heaven.

○ **The lost son.** The third story represents the climax: the parable of the lost boy. Of the three things that were lost – the sheep, the coin, the son – it might be expected that the son was by far the most valuable. Nevertheless, when the sheep was lost, there was a night-time search until it was found. When the coin was lost there was the search among the grime of the floor until it was found. *But when the son was lost there was no search.*

Why not?

○ Coins are nice shiny people, like Pharisees; they don't even know they're lost. They have no spiritual sense whatever and feel no spiritual need. They're lost and they don't know it.

○ Sheep know a little more than coins. They're rather like what the Pharisees called 'sinners' – the ordinary people – in Jesus' day. They knew they were lost but they didn't know what to do about it. They had some spiritual sense.

○ But the son knew he was lost – and he was glad of it! He knew the road

home, but he chose not to take it.

The story begins when the younger of two sons went to his father and said, 'I want my share of your money now. I'm off. I can't wait until you're dead!' The father employed servants and could have ordered them to bind the son and secure him in a locked room until he came to his senses. But that's not the way God works. And the Father, in this story, represents God. The first principle of God's government is freedom of choice; if someone wants to leave his home for a far country he is free to do so.

In the far country

In the far country the son felt that he'd exchanged a bicycle for a BMW! He could live life in the fast lane! He took the substance of life, squandered it, and went bust.

A famine arose; but the famine did not begin on the day the prodigal's bank balance registered red. It had been there in the background all the time. The economy of the far country made no provision for those who had run out of substance. It had no currency of its own or welfare system. The law of the jungle prevailed. When you'd run out of substance the far country said, 'Tough! Get lost!'

The far country has a place for lost sons and daughters. And it's the scrap heap.

He took his inheritance, squandered it – and went bust

The lost son ended up feeding pigs. He was so hungry that he even felt that he could eat the pigs' swill. Then, said Jesus, who was telling the story, 'He came to himself.' Suddenly he saw things clearly. In his father's home there were three categories of people: sons – part of the family, sharing in the father's possessions; slaves – who had security and were regarded as an extension of the family; hired servants – at the bottom of the social heap – who might be hired today and fired tomorrow.

In the pigsty the younger son said, 'Even the hired servants have enough to eat in my father's house, and to spare.'

Then he began to rehearse what he would do. He would return to his father's house. He would prostrate himself. And he would say, 'Father, I have sinned against heaven and against you. I am no longer worthy to be called your son.' All that was true enough. But he also planned to add, 'Make me like one of your hired men.' That meant he did not understand his father. He thought he could make up for the sins of the past by the good deeds of the future. That he could, in other words, *earn* his father's favour, make his own atonement. But we have already discovered that there is no do-it-yourself salvation. . . .

Come home to the Father

Here is how Jesus continues the story: ' "So he got up and went to his father. But while he was still a long way off, his father saw him and was filled with compassion for him; he ran to his son, threw his arms around him and kissed him. . . ." ' (Verses 19, 20.)

This has to be the most heartwarming picture of all. The father had never given up on his wayward son. Day after day his eyes had scanned the road from the far country, peering into every dust cloud for the shape of his returning son. When one day the shape appeared, he barely recognized it; unkempt, haggard, in rags. The scars of sin warp, distort and disfigure. But as soon as the light of recognition came into the father's eye '*he ran*'.

I have discussed this story with many Eastern fathers, Jewish and Arab. All have told me that they would never give this kind of reception to a returning wastrel. They would remain dignified and seated, avert their eyes and either permit the son to grovel before them or ignore him completely.

Jesus' revolutionary picture of God brought to life the idea of God as Father

Of course, Jesus knew all that. That is why this picture of God is so completely revolutionary. The Father ran, embraced and kissed the returning boy.

What happened to the prepared speech? First, the boy couldn't grovel before his father, because his father had grabbed him in a great bear hug.

The boy stank of the pigsty. But his father did not wait for him to be hosed down. He hugged his son. He knew that whatever his son had to say had better be said with his head on his father's shoulder.

It was the attitude of the father that broke the boy's heart and brought him to repentance. In the pigsty he had made a purely practical decision. When his head was on his father's shoulder everything changed. Ignoring the stench, the father placed the 'kiss of justification' upon his cheek, consigning his sins to oblivion.

The returning boy delivered the first part of his prepared speech, but not the second. In his father's arms he learned much about his limitless love and matchless grace. The second part of the speech he had prepared had said, in effect, 'Let me make my own atonement. Let my degradation continue. Let me atone for what I have done by what I will do.'

But the father would have none of it. He gave instructions to his servants: 'Quick! Bring the best robe and put it on him.' Having consigned the boy's sins to oblivion the father was giving him a robe that symbolized a righteousness that was not his own. 'Put a ring on his finger and sandals on his feet.' The ring symbolized restored authority, and sandals, worn only by family members, indicated that he was being accepted back as a son, not as a slave or a hired man.

God gives a party!

It was then that the father called a party. Whenever a sinner returns home, heaven is put on red alert, party-footing!

Not everyone was happy about this arrangement. There was an elder brother who had never left home. He heard the rumble of the party as he returned from the fields – and he was angry!

Returning sinners are justified by grace through faith (Rom. 5:1, 2). But it was the justification – as well as the party – that the elder brother couldn't handle. Jesus introduced the elder brother into the story to represent the Pharisees. They would rather wastrel sons didn't return but, if they did, they insisted that they earn acceptance by performance, achievement, hard work.

But we are justified by faith, not good works. And faith is not a 'good work'. To be justified by faith alone does not mean that God rewards our faith by justifying us. To be justified by faith alone is another way of saying that we're justified by Christ alone. Faith has no value in itself. The only value it has is in its object. Christ is the object. Christ is the treasure; faith is only the hand that grasps Him. Christ is the water of life; faith is only the mouth that drinks Him. Christ is the Lamb of God slain on the Cross; faith is only the eye that beholds Him. To say that we are justified by faith alone is another way of saying we're justified by Christ alone, saved by what Christ did for us on Calvary: He died the death we deserve.

Elder brothers – Pharisees – can't swallow that. Jesus turned on the Pharisees and said: ' "You are those who justify yourselves before men, but God knows your hearts." ' Luke 16:15, RSV. In other words, 'You can fool some of the people some of the time, but you can't fool God *any* of the time!' There is no do-it-yourself salvation.

The elder brother was angry and would not go in to the party (Luke 15:28). But his father came out to reason with him. The son said, in effect, 'Dad, I've kept all your commandments. Didn't want to! But I have! And this is how you repay me . . . .'

What did he *really* want to do?

He gives us an unwelcome insight into his secret desires by suggesting that his younger brother had wasted his livelihood with harlots (verse 30). But this is the only place that harlots are mentioned in the story! Perhaps that's what *he* would have preferred to have done!

The elder brother had done many of the right things, but from the wrong motives. Like the coin, he was lost but didn't know it. He could not accept his father's grace. Could not enter into his father's joy.

How did the story end? Did the prodigal stay home? Did the elder brother repent and embrace his father's Gospel?

You decide. The story is about you. Find yourself in one of the categories: a lost son or daughter still in the far country? A lost son or daughter still in the pigsty? A lost son or daughter on the way home? Receiving the father's embrace? In the family, post-party?

Or are you an elder brother? Never having strayed from home, but never having truly come home either – never having repented, never having lost your pride and self-sufficiency in the father's embrace.

But the father wants both lost sons and elder brothers to come home. The father's preferred ending: 'Rejoice with me! For these my sons were dead and are alive again, were lost and are found.'

And that has to be great good news – for lost sons, lost daughters – and elder brothers!

Praise God that His love *is* broader than the measure of men's minds!

> 'Could we with ink the ocean fill,
> Or were the skies of parchment made;
> Were every stalk on earth a quill,
> And every man a scribe by trade,
> To write the love of God above
> Would drain the ocean dry;
> Nor could the scroll contain the whole
> If stretched from sky to sky.'
> *F. E. Lehman.*

Would you rather be a party-goer or a party-pooper?

Great, good news! None better! Good news about the character of God, our wonderful, all-loving heavenly Father.

This is how God looks close up, in sharp focus. His arms outstretched in welcome. . . .

Secrets of a
happy marriage

Two institutions were created by God at the dawn of earth-time: marriage and the Sabbath. They are connected. Sabbath celebration causes us to take quality time out with our Maker – and with our mate! Through the Sabbath, our relationships with our God, our marriage partner and our children are kept alive, meaningful and vibrant.

But marriage is a seven-day-a-week business, and so is our relationship with God. Our relationships with God and with our spouse interrelate all the time. God Himself conducted the first wedding ceremony. And today, even though many marriages in Western countries break down – nearly half of all marriages in Britain end in divorce – few doubt God's view that a happy marriage is the best environment for ✪ both partners to achieve their full potential and know security deep down, and ✪ children to be reared in an atmosphere of security and emerge as balanced, achieving young people well equipped for life.

Marriage is for life, not just for Christmas!

One day in Eden

When God had completed the physical creation and pronounced it 'very good' – on the sixth day of creation week – He said, ' "Let us make man in our image, in our likeness, and let them rule over the fish of the sea and the birds of the air, over the livestock, over all the earth, and over all the creatures that move along the ground." ' Genesis 1:26.

The record continues: 'So God created man in his own image, in the image of God he created him; male and female he created them. . . .' (Verse 27.)

In the following chapter, details are given as to how God performed this miracle. After He had created Adam, He said, ' "It is not good for the man to be alone. I will make a helper suitable for him." ' (Chapter 2, verse 18.)

Imagine the scene when God, having created Adam and breathed life into him, then proceeded to create Eve. Adam's eyes must have opened wide, and his whole body responded with excitement! Was it possible for anything to be that beautiful? And there was Eve standing before him, physical proof that it was! Adam must have, at first, stood back in dumb admiration when he saw the wife God had made him; and then two sets of eyes locked on. . . . There was poetry in Adam's verbalized response to God and to Eve:

' "This is now bone of my bones
    and flesh of my flesh;
she shall be called 'woman',
    for she was taken out of man." ' (Verse 23.)

The older versions of the Bible call Adam and Eve either 'helpmeets' or 'helpmates'. Either way, it's a wonderful idea. Here were two people who, come what may, would stand side by side through whatever life might present them with – joys and sorrows.

Jesus sanctified marriage by performing His first miracle at a wedding service in Cana of Galilee. Much later, when the Pharisees came to catch Him out with questions about marriage, Jesus gave the institution His full-hearted support. ' "Is it lawful for a man to divorce his wife for any and every reason?" ' (Matthew 19:3) the Pharisees asked Jesus. He replied: ' "Haven't you read that at the beginning the Creator 'made them male and female', and said, 'For this reason a man will leave his father and mother and be united to his wife, and the two will become one flesh'? So they are no longer two, but one. Therefore what God has joined together, let man not separate." ' (Verses 4-6.)

Christ's great champion, Paul, used marriage as a metaphor for Christ's relationship with His Church: 'Husbands, love your wives, just as Christ loved the church and gave himself up for her . . . .' Ephesians 5:25, 26. Paul repeated the 'one flesh' teaching of Jesus and added, 'Each one of you also must love his wife as he loves himself, and the wife must respect her husband.' Verses 32 and 33.

The 'honeymoon phase' is an exciting voyage of discovery . . .

Phases of marriage

The experts tell us that a marriage goes through three different phases:

✪ During the honeymoon phase the couple feel that they know and understand each other. In courtship they have found pleasure in understanding and being understood. There has been an exciting voyage of discovery; the frankness of one has evoked the openness of the other. This dialogue carries over into marriage. They talk freely about essential, intimate, personal things. They thrill each time they discover one more thing they have in common.

This 'honeymoon phase' may last for weeks, months, or even years into marriage; the sense of spontaneous, mutual understanding may persist.

✪ Phase two generally occurs between the fifth and tenth years of marriage. Mutual understanding is no longer spontaneous. Indeed, it may cease to be mutual – or to exist at all. The sense of sameness gives way to an awareness of difference. Faults, obscured during the 'in love' period of early matrimony, make themselves painfully evident: selfishness, temper, greed, vulgarity. The 'I simply don't understand him/her' reaction begins to occur. With it may come the beginnings of withdrawal; perhaps abdication.

✪ Phase three will develop in the direction the previous phase has taken. If withdrawal and abdication have begun they may well continue. They are usually preceded by a period of scolding, imploring, maybe even threatening. Withdrawal and abdication indicate a progressive giving up in the struggle for happiness, and involve strong feelings of resentment, bitterness and rebellion. 'He's changed out of all recognition. I don't *know* him any more.' 'The violins stopped playing for us *years* ago.' 'I made a terrible mistake . . . .'

. . . but, after a time, the nature of the relationship changes

If the crisis has progressed this far – and without a strong undercurrent of mutual regard, a plethora of external pressures to provide a common cause, or a great deal of effective communication, it may have done – its upshot may take any one of a number of different forms. Divorce is just one. A cold war of unsettled areas of dispute is another. There may be a form of agreement in which one partner capitulates to the other and effectively gives up his right to an independent personality. Perhaps withdrawal will progress so far that each partner will organize his own life and become more and more secretive.

Even when the crisis is well advanced, however – and at any point before – partners may arrive at a mutually acceptable stable pattern for living. Whatever else is involved in this, the common denominator will be a courageous acceptance of reality: accepting one's partner as he or she is, and loving him or her for it.

Seven secrets of a happy marriage

A wedding is an event, but a marriage is an achievement. When the wide-eyed couple stand at the altar they have the easiest part over with. The hard part is two very different personalities adapting to one another in the twenty-four-hours-a-day, seven-days-a-week real world.

In a wedding service the pastor asks God's blessing on a marriage that will actually be made amid pots and pans, frantic financial fiascos, hectic work schedules, tensions, pressures and jangled nerves. Jesus said (Mark 10:8), ' " 'The two will *become* one flesh.' " ' Lots of people think He was talking about sex. He wasn't. That's why He used the word *become*. He knew that marriages are made over time in a hard-scrabble, brass-tacks environment. 'One flesh' is when the couple have achieved the adaptation of which sex is only the symbol.

So marriages are made over time, and tested by crises. Getting married is easy. But what are the secrets of *staying* married?

We've come up with seven you might like to think about.

1) Love. Falling in love is easy; but one of the greatest illusions of courtship is that love is self-sustaining. Paul Tournier says that love is an adventure and that the first law of adventure is that it needs constantly to be *reborn*.

Romantic love of the sort invented by novelists may not long outlive the honeymoon. Certainly, in a marriage that lasts, 'love' will mean something different after five years, and something different again after fifteen. In such a marriage love matures through constant rebirth. And this ongoing rebirth process depends on Christ and creativity.

The Bible passage that ministers like to quote on love is 1 Corinthians 13. They tend to pass over 1 Corinthians 7:3-5 because it embarrasses them. Here Paul has latched on to the 'ongoing' concept. He talks about the importance of husbands and wives *constantly* demonstrating their love for one another. He also talks about God's displeasure with marriage partners who are cold and withhold affection.

Love needs to be demonstrated. And demonstrating love can take many forms. Ellen White wrote a book about this around the time my grandfather was falling in love with my grandmother! 'Study to advance the happiness of each other,' she wrote. In other words: study each other's needs, wants, ways and preferences. 'Don't neglect the little attentions.' Sound advice. Both husband and wife need daily reassurance by word and deed that they are loved, and esteemed above all others. Love may die if it is not demonstrated.

It's not fate that destroys love; it's bad planning, lack of imagination and selfishness. If one or both halves of a couple feel foolish about expressing love in words, then they need to get over it. Much depends on it. And certainly deeds are as important as words; a surprise night out, a gift when it's not anybody's birthday. . . .

2) Communicate. 'Be kind and compassionate to one another, forgiving each other.' Ephesians 4:32. Here Paul the apostle has drawn the bottom line.

Communication is of the essence. The marriage manuals tell us there are five levels of communication:

✪ **Level 5** is shallow small-talk which leads to boredom. Husband returns from work. Wife is watching television. 'How was your day, dear?' she

Communication is what holds a marriage together, but it should be at Level 1

asks, her eyes not leaving the screen for an instant. He mumbles something she doesn't hear and, for a brief while, delves into his dumb brain for information that might form the basis of a question about *her* day. He gives up. She hasn't noticed.

●**Level 4** is exchanging facts; better than nothing, but not very meaningful.

●**Level 3** involves exposing thoughts and ideas and, therefore, involves a limited degree of vulnerability.

●**Level 2** is expressing feelings and emotions.

●**Level 1** is exchanging the heart's innermost secrets.

The message of the experts? Below level 3, you're in trouble!

Problems and crises are inevitable. Expect them. And when they come, talk them through. When there is an element of conflict never give your partner 'the silent treatment'. Silence can be the cruellest and most destructive of weapons. Even a few well-frozen words will thaw and melt away, but silence is glacial. If you're hurt or angry don't keep it bottled up, but remember: Never believe anything your mate says when he or she is angry. When anger takes over, reason is suspended. Verbalize problems without using emotive words. Practise 'active listening'; listen for *feelings* as well as words.

Settle outstanding problems before bedtime. 'Never go to bed angry – don't give the devil that sort of foothold.' Ephesians 4:26, 27, Phillips.

3) Responsibility. We are responsible to two marriage partners – our mate and our Maker. For every act done to our mate in the tender relationship of marriage we shall have to give an account to a God who will countenance no injustice, and no violation of the sacrament of love.

4) Unity. The old wedding service used to include the phrase 'the twain shall be one'. A startled bride once interrupted her wedding by blurting out '*Which* one?' The answer has to be: Neither. It is a new oneness that is established to which both partners make their contribution. But that does not mean that we lose our personal identity in this new relationship. This balance can be a hard one to work out.

A church wedding is bound to throw up the words, 'The husband is the head of the wife.' Ephesians 5:23. The new husband smiles as if to say, 'Advantage, me. Yes?' *No.* The next phrase in the text is: '*as Christ is the head of the church*'. The Bible calls for a special kind of leadership in marriage. There are no bosses. It is the leadership of love; and a leadership without domination, direct or indirect. It involves a complete dedication to the welfare of the other partner.

5) Privacy. Lack of it can damage the beauty of a marriage relationship. There is a sacred circle around a marriage that should be kept intact. No relative or friend, however close, has the right to break that circle.

Relatives and friends come as guests to the home, not as experts on curtaining, carpeting, furnishing, finance or child discipline.

Nor has the husband or wife the right to break the circle by discussing his or her mate with others.

This may be the right place to say that the Chinese word for war is made up of the symbols of two women and of the symbol for one roof. . . .

The leadership of love – not domination – maintains the unity of the Christian marriage

6) Time. This is one to watch out for when a marriage is a little way down the road. There is such a thing as becoming so absorbed with others or other commitments – even hobbies – that a marriage partner stops spending quality time with his or her mate. Then, when they *do* finally meet up for a while, the communication system seems to have been tampered with

When a marriage partner stops spending quality time with his or her mate, trouble is brewing

and the thoughts of both members of the partnership are elsewhere. One six-year study of married couples turned up the information that even those who considered their relationships 'moderately happy' only spent twenty-seven-and-a-half minutes a week in shared activities and conversation.

We need time, ingenuity, creativity – and Christ. Without Him our love will vibrate through the house like noisy gongs and clanging symbols. With Him our duet may approximate to harmony; at best be a little bit of heaven on earth by the good Lord's grace.

7) Heavenly help. Let's give the last word to the lady who wrote down her inspired thoughts around the time my grandfather was falling in love with my grandmother. Remember? Ellen G. White:

'Make Christ first and last and best in everything. . . .

'Men and women can reach God's ideal for them if they will take Christ as their helper. What human wisdom cannot do, His grace will accomplish for those who give themselves to Him in loving trust. His providence can unite hearts in bonds that are of heavenly origin. Love will not be a mere exchange of soft and flattering words. The loom of heaven weaves with warp and woof finer, yet more firm, than can be woven by the looms of earth. The result is not a tissue fabric but a mixture that will bear wear and test and trials. Heart will be bound to heart in a golden bond of love that is enduring.'

Yes, even the success of our marriage is dependent upon our relationship with God, as is everything else of importance in our lives. This leads us by a natural process to the vital importance of spending quality time with the King of kings. . . .

God's Good News

Quality time with God

One great thing about being a Christian is that you can spend quality time with the most wonderful and lovable – as well as powerful – Person in the whole universe.

The God of all glory became Man in Jesus, lived in a town like yours, was tempted as you are tempted, faced many of the problems you face, then, a few weeks after His resurrection, returned to His home in heaven.

The result?

'We have a great High Priest who has gone into the very presence of God – Jesus, Son of God. Our High Priest is not one who cannot feel sympathy for our weaknesses. On the contrary, we have a High Priest who was tempted in every way that we are, but did not sin. Let us be brave, then, and approach God's throne, where there is grace. There we will receive mercy and find grace to help us just when we need it.' Hebrews 4:14-16, GNB.

Amazing news —
the God of the
universe wants to
be your friend!

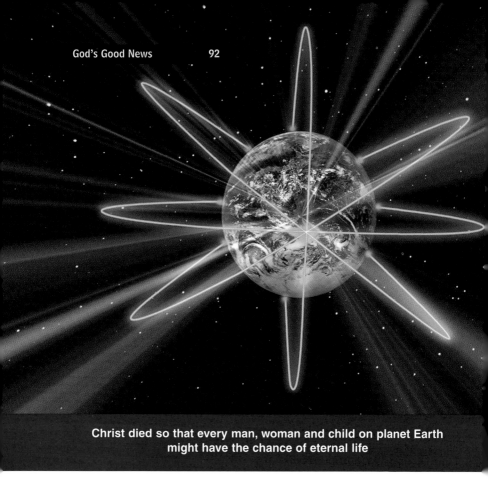

Christ died so that every man, woman and child on planet Earth might have the chance of eternal life

Cosmic Mission Control

What a marvellous picture! At Cosmic Mission Control is One who created us and loved us enough to die in our place. One who can empathize with us when we face temptation, crisis, trauma, pain, loss. He knows all about us, but loves us anyway; and His love, like His mercy and kindness, is everlasting (Ps. 100:5; Isa. 54:8; Jer. 31:3).

No wonder we are urged to approach with boldness the One who is all loving. He is interested in every aspect of our lives; as our High Priest, He deals with our sin problems, then, with the Father and the Holy Spirit, concerns Himself with every physical, social, intellectual and spiritual challenge that comes our way.

Such a wonderful Being as our triune God – Father, Son, Holy Spirit – is surely worth getting to know. How do we get to know Him?

○ **Prayer.** The Christian without a meaningful prayer life will not be a Christian for long. *With* a meaningful prayer life he can be equal to anything circumstances throw at him. No burden is so great He will not shoulder it for him. No problem is too petty to draw to His attention. Prayer is the opening of the heart to a Friend who is, at once, all loving and all powerful. There need be no set posture or place – though a regular habit of prayer is essential – and Cosmic Mission Control never sleeps (Ps. 121:3, 4).

○ **Bible study.** You don't have to be a scholar to study the Bible – though when you start studying it you might well become one! But shovelling information is not the point of Bible study. Remember, the Bible is 'God-breathed'; as such, it is a source of power and enlightenment. How so? In the Bible God reveals Himself. Begin reading with the gospels and the Acts. Read the story; get to know Him. Then tackle the New Testament letters that explain the Good News. After that, you'll be ready to graduate to the Old Testament. Set aside time every day for Bible study; that way your life will become a partnership with the only Friend who will never let you down.

○ **Worship.** We begin to resemble what or whom we worship or prize most. Everyone worships someone or something. Augustine said, 'There is a God-shaped blank in everyone'; and if we do not worship the wonderful God of the Good News Book, then the demi-gods of stage, screen and sport take His place, or maybe the material things we spend our lives collecting. Everyone worships; and once exposed to the Good News you will experience an irresistible urge to worship God. The Bible takes the view that worship is best done in company (Heb. 10:25) and involves the elements of music and biblical exposition.

What a privilege to begin, end and spend each day with the One who both created and redeemed us!

What a comfort to know that Cosmic Mission Control is tuned in to our every need and that we have an all-powerful Friend whose love is limitless.

Law in eclipse

Have you ever wondered what God feels as He watches the great out-splurge of evil that constitutes 'the main points of the news' on a typical day?

'God seems so far away,' said somebody. But guess who moved? Not God. The last century has seen a major shift away from prayer, from the Bible, from worship – from God.

But we need something more to explain what is happening in today's world. Every character in every plot, every situation in every scene, every line of the entire script of today's story is stained with the weeping poison of that characteristically modern viewpoint that guilt is to be healed by lowering standards, *that we need no law*. Personality problems, home problems, marriage problems and juvenile problems, violence in the classroom, in the streets, in the tower blocks and in the living rooms, any and every social problem of this great *Play For Today* shouts out the bankruptcy of that life-view that has sought to break down law and authority. And, most importantly, the divine Authority of God's law.

Eternal principles

Sadly, modern theologians have to accept their share of the blame for the breakdown of law, because many have asserted that God's stone-written record

Space flight is only possible when scientists adhere strictly to the laws of physics. Society will only work successfully when its members adhere to the laws governing behaviour: God's moral law

of ten eternal principles of right was 'nailed to the cross'. No! What was 'nailed to the cross' was the collective weight of our sins. Obedience to God's law is the love response we owe to the One who saved us. The pardon we receive through Calvary does not give us licence to break God's law; it only deepens our obligation to keep it (Rom. 6:14, 15).

God's ten great commands are a giant dam holding back the tidal wave of violence, hurt, unhappiness, filth and depravity. Remove one block and the flood tide rolls through our society, carrying all before it. Break one commandment and you have broken them all (James 2:10).

Aside from those who believe that God's law no longer applies, some Christians, though accepting nine of God's ten eternal principles, ignore one of them. Not deliberately, perhaps, but possibly out of ignorance or because they do not believe that it is important. The commandment they neglect is the fourth. Perhaps God foresaw this state of affairs, for He commenced this commandment with the imperative – *Remember*.

And what does God invite us to 'Remember'? To spend quality time with Him one day out of seven. To be specific:

'Remember the Sabbath day, to keep it holy. Six days shalt thou labour, and do all thy work: but the seventh day is the Sabbath of the Lord thy God . . . .' Exodus 20:8-10, KJV.

God is, apparently, particular. Particular, among other things, about the day on which He is to be worshipped.

The pressures and distractions of the modern world have caused a major erosion of true Sabbath worship, regardless of the day – the specific day – God said to remember. And this has had catastrophic consequences for another God-ordained institution. Only two institutions were originated by God in Eden: the Sabbath – and the family.

God is particular about the day on which He is to be worshipped

The **forgotten** day

Sindy. Life was hell on wheels for Sindy. Pressured by her teachers to score high at university. Pressured by parents to live up to the family name, be cute, bright and sparkling like the neighbours' kids. Pressured by peers to 'do drugs'. Pressured by boys to 'do sex'.

So many things locked up in her heart. So much to give. No one to receive. No one to listen. Mum and Dad caught up in their own busy, lifestyle: both working long hours; nights out with friends. No time for Sindy. Her problems would have to stay locked up. Once complained to her mum that nobody 'communicated' in their family – and Mum gave her the phone number of a good doctor!

And Sindy couldn't escape from this house of strangers. Her own flesh and blood; but strangers for all that.

Matt and Louise. Matt was going places – fast. Peck on the cheek and off at a fast gallop to grab the commuter train for the city. There were wage scales to be climbed, promotions to be fought for, mortgages to be paid, deals to be done, worlds to be conquered.

Home at 7.30pm. Turn on the telly; helping of second-hand adventure, fantasy, might ease his mind of the nerve-stretching stress, pull his thoughts away from today's quota of aggro.

Scratch meals; caught a cheese burger from McDonalds for lunch. Vindaloo from the take-away for tea.

Turned off the television when they mentioned 'executive burn-out'. Didn't like the sound of that.

Tossed and turned all night. Not enough relaxation. Not to worry; there'd be time down the boozer with the lads at the weekend.

What was Louise fussing about? Never got to see him? Didn't seem the same man she'd married? Didn't spend enough time with the kids? What kids? He'd spent a small fortune on computer games to keep them quiet, hadn't he?

Why be a misery, Louise? Stick with it for a couple of years and I'll have powered up to the hot seat. And then . . . .

From opposite ends of the breakfast table they wondered what was clotting their rapport these days.

Steve. Audi, his right foot flat on the floor. Nought to sixty in 9.4 seconds. Top speed 150 mph. Stereo full blast – all eight speakers. Executive briefcase on the back seat. Glanced in the rear-view mirror. That ninety-tooth smile, gleaming white teeth, tools of the trade, right? Sell Centre Point to any hick from the sticks with those sincere teeth.

Tracey wanted to talk. But there had been no time for all that. He took her to Round Table, right? Couldn't she make friends in the neighbourhood, or something? Much more hassle and he'd trade her in for a deluxe model. Like Jane at the office . . . .

Home at 8.30pm. No Tracey. Just a note and no forwarding address. At 8.47pm, or so they told the Coroner, £30,000-worth of *Vorsprung durch Technik* hit a motorway bridge support at somewhat in excess of 100 mph.

Lucy and Sean. It can be great being 13 like Lucy or 8 like Sean. But it depends. Often Dad's face looked pale. He sat slumped over the video, miserable. It wasn't the same between Dad and Mum any more. They'd heard Dad say so. And Grandad had said plenty more: When *he* was young, families went together, *did* things together. Lucy and Sean liked the sound of that. All the family together – in the park, off on a ride; it really didn't matter where or what. But *together*. Mum said there was no time for all that. She wanted Lucy to be 'liberated' like her, but Lucy wasn't struck on that. A loner at school, often crying; teachers couldn't make her out. She was drawn apart, closed in a violent silence. An under-achiever. And Sean? He was never home. What was the point?

Whatever happened to families?

The increased incidence of divorce, suicide, kids on the prowl – is there a pattern?

All-absorbing careers.

Television and video to avoid the embarrassment of communication.

Every member isolated, his life vacuum-packed, sealed in with his own private weather.

End results?

Most of the statistics that make headlines.

AIDS – mega-epidemic proportions. Divorces – up. Suicides – up. The statistics of violence, mugging, kids on the prowl – up. Incidence of duodenal ulcers and coronaries – up. Schoolgirl pregnancies – up. Number of teenage runaways – up. And the extent and intensity of things like loneliness and misery cannot be measured.

How to get back to the simplicity of happy homes and secure families? How to cope with the pressures of life in the twenty-first century? How to be a mum, dad, child – *human being* – these days *and stay happy?*

Why couldn't somebody have invented a day – say just twenty-four hours in a seven-day week – when the pressures would be off? When the workaday week would be forgotten. Shut out. A day that would liberate everyone from the madding, materialistic society – the tyranny of the world of *things*. One day in the week when a man need not feel small, anonymous, a face in the crowd, but have a sense of his significance, identity, belonging, roots.

One day a week when a man, rushed off his hurrying feet on a weekday, could relax and communicate with, *enjoy*, his wife, his children, his family, his friends, his partners in the business of living. One day a week when, instead of *exploiting* God's creation, he could *experience* the rest and peace of *appreciating* it.

Was it too much to ask that there should be one day a week when a man could, so to speak, recharge his batteries: renew his spirit, revitalize his flagging physique, spark his mind into creative activity, and find joy in his family?

Ought not someone to have invented such a day?

Like God, for example?

Of course, God did. Way back. Remember – just two institutions founded in Eden? One of them the Sabbath? They went together, the Sabbath and the family. *God sanctified both.*

In His ten stone-written rules of right and justice, God said, 'Remember the Sabbath . . . .' But the day God said to remember has become the forgotten day.

Jesus did not forget it. He said He was 'Lord of the Sabbath'.

His disciples didn't forget it. When Christian missionaries went to the limits of the known world, they took the Sabbath with them.

But through the hurrying centuries it has become the forgotten day. The world has become one vast supermarket. Everyone shoving trolleys that won't go straight. Grabbing, grasping everything in sight. Heaping up their mountains of *things*.

Because the day has been forgotten, real values have been forgotten – and God has been forgotten, too.

And life has become hell on wheels – for Sindy.

A fast track to divorce for Matt and Louise, with nervous breakdowns and coronaries just milestones *en route*.

A seven-day week, top speed, sound-bursting mayhem to suicide for Steve.

Warped, mind-blown, loveless, lonely childhood for Lucy and Sean.

All because law is in eclipse.

All because the day God said to remember became – the forgotten day.

The case of the
overlooked law

esus habitually kept the Sabbath, and each Saturday would find Him in the synagogue (Luke 4:16; Mark 6:1-4). Nazareth's carpenter shop would be full of bustle and business six days a week, but on Saturday it would be closed and quiet. The Sabbath, Saturday, was a family time, a worship time for the carpenter's family in Nazareth.

Jesus, Lord of the Sabbath

One of the main thrusts of Jesus' teaching was a reformation of the Sabbath. In His day, the church establishment had so many rules about Sabbath observance that they had made the Sabbath a burden. Jesus sought to restore God's ideal of the Sabbath as a 'delight' when men and women, boys and girls, would find their 'joy in the Lord' (Isa. 58:13, 14). By word and action, Jesus taught the people that God's blessings would be poured out when sacred time was spent helping the sick and under-privileged, and enjoying God's creation – as well as in worship (Matt. 12:1-14; Mark 2:27, 28; 6:1-4; Luke 6:1-11; 13:10-17; 14:1-14; John 5:1-15; 7:21-24. See Isaiah 58). Sadly, Jesus' Sabbath crusade brought Him into nose-on conflict with the church authorities who, as a direct result, began to plot His death (Matt. 12:1-14).

What would have been the point of expending so much time and effort to reform an institution – the Sabbath – if it was about to be 'done away with' at the cross?

During the week prior to His crucifixion, Jesus, looking down the corridor of time to AD70, told His disciples that Jerusalem would be destroyed. To those of His followers who would be living in Jerusalem, He detailed signs that would indicate that the destruction was near. When they recognized those signs, they were to flee the city. ' "Pray that your flight will not take place in the winter or on the Sabbath," ' Jesus urged them (Matt. 24:20. See also verses 3-20).

Clearly, Jesus envisaged His followers observing the Sabbath long after the resurrection.

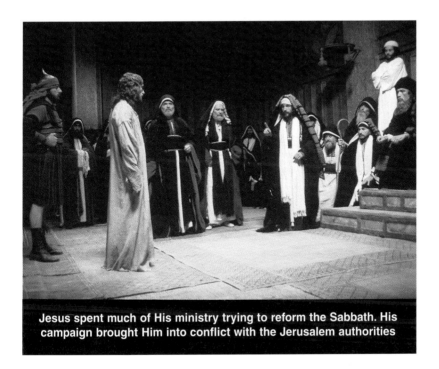

Jesus spent much of His ministry trying to reform the Sabbath. His campaign brought Him into conflict with the Jerusalem authorities

So what happened to the Sabbath?

That was what Judge Alan C. Kay, Chief Judge of the United States District Court of Hawaii, wanted to know. He was a Sunday-keeping Christian but had just discovered that, in contrast to his Church, Jesus had observed the Saturday Sabbath. Why was it that with close on two billion Christians in the world only about ten million of them followed Jesus' example in Sabbath observance?

Kay decided to use his lawyers' training to find some answers. He told his story in *Liberty*, a magazine with a circulation of 700,000, read by legislators at state and federal level, as well as by the legal profession, throughout the USA. (*Liberty*, volume 88, number 1.)

'The inspired instruction on how to resolve such an issue was clear – by examining the Scriptures daily to see "whether those things were so" (Acts 17:11, KJV),' wrote Kay. 'So I studied the Word.'

As a lawyer and judge he began with the law itself. He discovered that in the fourth of the ten commandments 'the Lord blessed the Sabbath day and made it holy' and commanded mankind 'to keep it holy' (Exodus 20:8-11).

The legislative history of the Sabbath, noted Kay, began at creation: 'And on the seventh day God ended his work which he had made; and he rested on the seventh day from all his work. . . . And God blessed the seventh day, and sanctified it.' Genesis 2:2, 3, KJV. 'To sanctify', noted the judge, 'meant "to set apart for holy use" '.

But the judge's lawyer's brain continued to ask questions; Does it matter whether *we* follow God's command? That's when he discovered that the apostle John directly linked our love of God with our obedience to Him: 'For this is the love of God, that we keep his commandments.' 1 John 5:3, KJV.

God was, and is, particular. He had singled out the seventh day, blessed it and made it holy – as a celebration of creation. The judge discovered that the New Testament emphasized the role of Christ in creation, stating that 'all

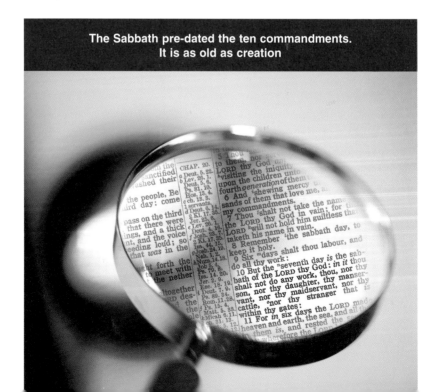

**The Sabbath pre-dated the ten commandments.
It is as old as creation**

things were created by him (Christ), and for him' (Col. 1:16; cf John 1:3; Heb. 1:2). Jesus confirmed that He is 'Lord . . . of the Sabbath' (Mark 2:28).

'One doesn't need to be an attorney,' wrote Judge Kay, 'to know that laws can change. Legislatures not only change laws but even abolish them . . . .' The judge began a most thorough investigation of Scripture to discover whether the Sabbath commandment had ever been repealed. What he discovered was a promise from Jesus Himself that 'while heaven and earth endure not one iota or one projection of a letter will be dropped from the law'; that Jesus came, not to annul or abolish the law, but to demonstrate how to keep it (Matt. 5:17-20, *The Modern Language Bible*).

Noting that those who lived in the love of the Father were those who kept His commandments (John 15:10), the Judge began to dwell on the clause *'while heaven and earth endure'*. Pretty comprehensive; totally conclusive. That's how he saw it. The clause also reminded him of an Old Testament passage right at the end of the prophecy of Isaiah. In prophetic mode, Isaiah had been looking to a time beyond time. A central element of the picture painted by the prophet was that 'from one Sabbath to another, all mankind' would come and worship God (Isa. 66:23).

The judge was hot on the trail, and becoming fascinated by his quest. 'All mankind' did not mean just Jews; it meant *everyone*. Well, it would, wouldn't it? he reasoned. Since the Sabbath originated in Eden, the Sabbath predated the birth of the first Jew by thousands of years!

Because the law was 'holy, and just, and good' (Rom. 7:12, KJV), it could not be done away with; and since it could not be done away with, wrote Judge Kay, 'God sent His own Son in a human body to pay our penalty for law breaking.' Pursuing Paul, the judge discovered that part of the 'in Christ Jesus' experience was 'not [to] live according to the sinful nature' but, through the indwelling Spirit, to make every endeavour to live up to 'the righteous requirements of the law' (Rom. 8:3, 4).

'It is sometimes erroneously said that Jesus never mentioned the Sabbath commandment,' wrote Judge Kay. 'More accurately, it can be said that He never disputed the continued existence of the Sabbath, nor the day on which it was observed. That the Sabbath was the seventh day was acknowledged.

The only issue in the New Testament is how the Sabbath should be observed. . . . His emphasis on proper Sabbath observance was a significant factor in His persecution.'

Short of changing the Sabbath from the seventh day to the first day at His crucifixion, Christ's first 'act' after His crucifixion on Friday was to rest in the tomb over the Sabbath. Jesus arose on Sunday, the first day of the week (Luke 23:50-56; 24:1-9), but nowhere instructed Christians to celebrate His resurrection by worshipping on Sunday. To the contrary, the apostle Paul had presented baptism as the commemoration of the death, burial and resurrection of Jesus (Rom. 6:1-11). Jesus had taught explicitly that we should remember Him until His return by participating in Communion (1 Cor. 11:23-26). Jesus, discovered Judge Kay, prescribed a new *way* of remembering Him, but never prescribed a new *day* for worshipping Him.

The unalterable covenant

After His death Jesus *did* open His disciples' minds to 'understand the Scriptures' (Luke 24:45); but you can search the Scriptures in vain for evidence that either Christ or any of His apostles abolished the Sabbath or changed it to another day. In Christ's Great Commission to take the good news to every nation on earth, He included the words 'teaching them to observe all things that I have commanded you' (Matt. 28:19, 20, RAV).

What were the commands of Jesus regarding the Sabbath that we should teach others to observe?

✪ He taught that it was lawful to do good on the Sabbath. ✪ He taught that He was Lord of the Sabbath. ✪ He taught that the Sabbath was made for man, not man for the Sabbath (Mark 2:27).

After the resurrection, the apostles, together with their Jewish and Gentile converts, continued to observe the Sabbath. (See Acts 13:42-44; 16:13; 18:4.) At the Council of Jerusalem, James, the brother of Jesus, noted in his address that Moses was read in the synagogues every Sabbath (Acts 15:21). The apostles taught Christian converts to obey the commandments – including the Sabbath commandment. 'What matters,' said Paul, 'is keeping the commandments of God.' 1 Corinthians 7:19, NASB.

From Sabbath to Sunday

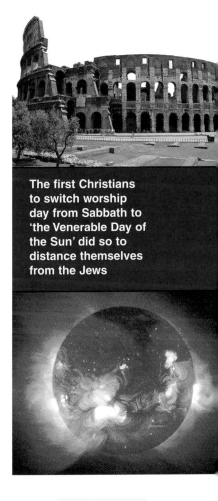

The first Christians to switch worship day from Sabbath to 'the Venerable Day of the Sun' did so to distance themselves from the Jews

As you can imagine, with all the evidence in, Judge Alan C. Kay became one of the ten million seventh-day Sabbath-keepers the world around.

Of course, one thing continued to fascinate him. How did the situation come about whereby the majority of Christians switched from Saturday to Sunday worship?

A lot of detective work has been done in this area. Dr Samuele Bacchiocchi was awarded his doctorate for his dissertation *From Sabbath to Sunday*, published by the Pontifical Gregorian University Press, Rome, in 1977. Bacchiocchi left no historical stone unturned. He demonstrated that the first Christian congregations to switch to Sunday did so well after the death of the apostles. Further, that for several centuries many congregations either continued to worship on the seventh-day Sabbath or worshipped on both Sabbath and Sunday.

The first congregations to make the switch did so, apparently, in order to distance themselves from the Jews. However, the major change came in the era following the conversion of the Emperor Constantine in AD321 when Christianity merged with paganism by adopting many of the Emperor's pre-Christian practices. After all, Constantine had been converted from sun worship to Christianity. It was therefore not surprising that he ordered all subjects, except farmers, to 'rest on the venerable day of the sun'.

Not until the fourth century did it occur to anyone to explain Sunday sacredness by reference to the 'day of resurrection'.

Who **changed** the **Sabbath?**

The Roman Catholic Church for hundreds of years has made the claim to have changed the Sabbath. More than that: the Roman Church chides Protestants, who profess to follow the Bible, for accepting a day of worship owing its sanctity only to Roman authority.

From Peter Geiermann's *Converts' Catechism of Catholic Doctrine* (1957):

Q. Which is the Sabbath day?

A. Saturday is the Sabbath day.

Q. Why do we observe Sunday instead of Saturday?

A. We observe Sunday instead of Saturday because the Catholic Church

The Gospel Sabbath

The seventh-day Sabbath is a symbol of both creation and redemption.

What a wonderful day the sixth day of creation week must have been! At the end of it, as He ushered in sacred time with the glory of the first sunset, it was as if God said to Adam, 'Adam, behold this wonderful world, full of objects animate and inanimate, which call for admiration; but beware – none of them, nor all of them, not even Eve can satisfy you. For you were made for Me; your heart can find rest only in Me, your Source.' And God invited Adam to spend that first Sabbath with Him, and that was God's acted-out invitation to everyone to find rest, joy and strength in Him.

On the sixth day of redemption week, Good Friday, Jesus cried, 'It is finished', and then rested. He could have risen the next day, but He chose to rest in death that Sabbath, as He had rested each Sabbath of His earthly life. The writer of the Hebrews (4:9) explained the significance of this; 'There remains, then, a Sabbath-rest for the people of God . . . .' The word translated 'Sabbath rest' is *sabbatismos* which means Sabbath-*like* rest. When the transferred the solemnity from Saturday to Sunday.

The Christian Sabbath, second edition (first published in *Catholic Mirror* in 1893): 'The Catholic Church for over 1,000 years before the existence of a Protestant, by virtue of her divine mission, changed the day from Saturday to Sunday.' (Page 29.)

Again from *The Christian Sabbath*: 'But the Protestant says: How can I receive the teachings of an apostate Church? How, we ask, have you managed to receive her teaching all your life, *in direct opposition* to your recognized teacher, the Bible, on the Sabbath question?. . . The Christian Sabbath [the author means Sunday] is therefore *to this day* the acknowledged offspring of the Catholic Church. . . . without a word of remonstrance from the Protestant world.' (Pages 29-31.)

sinner accepts the finished redemption accomplished for him on Calvary by Christ, he can 'enter into rest'. His sins are atoned for. He can abandon all efforts to achieve salvation – and receive the assurance of *God's* salvation.

Sabbath is a symbol of our peace in Christ through His completed work of atonement.

On a weekly basis, the Sabbath reminds us of this: We must cease from trust in our own works, so continually stained by sin, and enter into His rest. Entering into – accepting – Sabbath rest symbolizes our abandonment of salvation by effort, our acceptance of salvation offered by Christ and our entry into the experience of assurance.

Celebrated as it should be, the Sabbath is a coming of day into night, summer into winter, life into death, eternity into time.

Ideally, the Sabbath should be no less than this: the beginning of eternal life and heaven in the here-and-now world. The ultimate in quality time with God.

If you could
ask God one question . . .

What would it be?

Having read about the God who impacts into the Christian's life through prayer, through Scripture and through worship, *you* might begin to ask, 'But where is this God when we are hurting?' Having grasped the meaning of the marvellous gift of the Sabbath, through which God pours peace into a frantic, stressed-up world, *you* may ask: 'But how can I reconcile this God with the world around me – riven by wars, seared by suffering, faint with famine, shrieking in pain?'

A newspaper ran an opinion poll: 'If you could ask God one question what would it be?' The question was put to 1,894 people. The responses were all published.

Among them were the expected jokers: 'How can I win the national lottery?' 'Why wasn't I born rich?' 'Why do you make human beings so clever, and why are they so stupid in a lot of their actions?' But responses like these were untypical.

The typical question included two elements: real concern about the problems of the world; anger and frustration with God for allowing them or not tackling them.

Nine tenths of the questions addressed to God via the National Opinion Poll Organization, boiled down, would have been: 'WHY SUFFERING?'

Who is responsible?

Significantly, the Bible's oldest book struggles with the 'Who is responsible?' question. It was named after its central character: Job. Job was disturbed by God's silence when he was suffering. He could not reconcile the God he worshipped with the calamities he endured. He was angry with God and demanded answers. But the book of Job draws aside the curtain and reveals the unseen world . . . .

In this pre-Calvary world, the great controversy between good and evil was unresolved. A war had taken place in heaven and Satan, along with one

If God is all-powerful, why suffering? And why is it that the vulnerable suffer the most?

third of the heavenly host, had been cast out. By falling for Satan's primal lies the first humans had aligned earth with his evil empire. Evil angels infested the planet. Job, fiercely loyal to God, was being put to the test by the forces of evil. Satan's purpose was to destroy Job. God's purpose in permitting Job to be tried was to refine his character and to mature him with the eternal perspective of earth's great patriarch in view. Among other things, Job needed to learn that his great wealth did not make him independent of the God who had created him and permitted him to amass wealth. He also had to learn that God has no favourites.

Job lived through a dark night of the soul. All those who came to him and expounded their pocket philosophies to explain his plight only made things worse. And we find Job looking heavenward and shrieking, 'WHY?' (See Job 10:3.)

At length, Job heard God's voice through the whirlwind. God answered Job's question with questions – eighty in all! The questions concerned earthly things and natural phenomena. God was saying two things to Job by these questions. Firstly, 'Look, Job, you don't understand earthly things; how can you expect to understand heavenly things? Your grasp is limited. Your brain can grip only a fraction of the facts. One day, when we meet face to face, you will know all.' Secondly, God was saying, 'Job, you trust me with the things of earth and time; trust me with the great spiritual questions that will affect your eternity, and the eternity of others.'

You were born into a world that was choked with evil. The horrors that are beamed into our living rooms daily through the television news represent the outworking of evil in the world and the consequences of the wrong choices made by men and women. *Your Health in Your Hands,* by R. J. B. Willis, begins with the assertion that 74 per cent of all deaths in Western countries are caused by cardiovascular disease and cancer. Further, that in the majority of cases these deaths are preventable.

C. S. Lewis asserted that four-fifths of human suffering is self-inflicted; that the major diseases are caused by too much food and too little activity.

Who pushed you in? It may have been the devil himself. It may have been some politician whom you supported. It may have been one of the men of wealth and power who, through their wrong choices, exploit and help to render the earth uninhabitable. You may have been pushed as a result of the wrong choices of those somewhat closer to you.

And there is always a chance that you might have jumped . . . .

Questioning and trusting

'How *can* there be a God and the world be as it is?' demanded the man sitting next to me as the train sliced through the city slums. The 'why' question is as old as sin; because pain is the same age. In his personal agony, Jeremiah asked God, 'Why is my pain unending and my wound grievous and incurable? Will you be to me like a deceptive brook, like a spring that fails?' Jeremiah 15:18.

**How can there be a God and the world be as it is?
Is It God's fault?**

Martin Luther said that for all of us there are days when faith trembles in the balance, and we ask, 'Is it true?'

Christians have been wrestling with the WHY question for twenty centuries. Every Christian has known pain; the only way to avoid it is to die young. And, as with Job in *his* pain, there are two things we need to learn:

⚙ First, there are some questions that can be answered only when we reach the heavenly country; until then, we do not even understand the questions we are asking – and our limited brains could never grasp God's answers. Only God sees the whole problem. If we had the mind of God, we'd *be* God. We must be content to know somewhat less than the Omniscient One.

⚙ Second, we need to learn to trust. On the night of His betrayal, Jesus said to His disciples, 'What I do thou knowest not now; but thou shalt know hereafter.' John 13:7, KJV. Accepting *that* has to be the bottom line of our trust.

Job emerged out of *his* dark tunnel when he realized that his questions had been asked out of ignorance (42:3) and that, for the time being, he must be content to await patiently the disclosure of the full story when he would meet his living Redeemer at the resurrection of the righteous.

Even Jeremiah, surrounded by the smouldering ruins of Jerusalem, came to view God's dealings with him in a positive light: 'Because of the Lord's great love we are not consumed, for His compassions never fail. They are new every morning; great is your faithfulness . . . .' Lamentations 3:22-24.

Five
perspectives on pain

So, after twenty centuries of agonizing over the problem of pain, what has the Christian Church learned?

1) *If you believe that God is a God of love, you have one problem: the problem of evil. If you do not believe that God is love, you have a million problems.*

For every thousand people who raise the question, 'Why is there evil?' no one raises the far bigger question, 'Why is there good?'

What make the newspaper headlines are always the variations from the norm: calamities, atrocities, evil doings. Virtue, fulfilled lives, healthy people, loving families and incident-free travel do not make news. The norm of life is good: daily food, the ordinary use of our faculties, the unhindered enjoyment of our lives. The greatest blessings of life exist in profusion. But, because they are the norm, they are unremarkable. They indicate the existence of God and good in the world.

2) *The universe is based on the rule of law; life and order depend upon it.*

All worthwhile things depend upon the reliability of natural law. Without it there would be no agriculture, no science and no life. Yet every natural law has a flip side. For example, the law of gravity that keeps us on the surface of the planet also dictates

'Why is there evil?' is a big question. 'Why is there good?' is a bigger one

that when we jump from the thirteenth floor of a tower block we fall to our death.

God is a God of law. He made a universe, not a multiverse. Though, from time to time, for reasons beyond our comprehension, God may choose to set aside natural law and perform a miracle.

3) *Freedom of choice is the first principle of the government of God.*

God gave man the gift of free choice; man was made a free agent, not a robot. By giving man freedom, God, in effect, placed limitations on His own freedom of action. Man must take the consequences of his own wrong choices, and the wrong choices of others. It is worth while remembering that man, not God, invented bows and arrows, bullets, bayonets, bombs and intercontinental ballistic missiles.

4) *In certain circumstances, suffering and pain may serve a purpose.*

C. S. Lewis called pain, 'God's megaphone'. Does it ever occur to us that God may have permitted pain or distress as a means of gaining our attention – after exhausting all other means? Be that as it may, it is a fact that whether we emerge from life's hard knocks bitter or better for the experience will depend on the attitude we adopt towards them.

Mark Twain's childhood was spent in poverty. When he was 20 he watched his brother burn to death in an explosion on a Mississippi river boat. When he married, his first child died soon after birth. He was responsible for the death of his second child; he left her pram carriage out in the snow uncovered. The third child died because of his carelessness; he let go of the pushchair at the top of a hill . . . . Before his death, Twain wrote a bitter book full of hatred of life, faith and God. Mark Twain was made bitter by his trials.

John Donne suffered many reversals, too. Every career he turned his hand to ended in failure and debt. Until, that is, he was ordained to the Gospel ministry in 1615. But that was when his wife died, leaving him with seven children! Five years later he became Dean of St Paul's; thousands travelled for miles to hear his great sermons. Then he began to display the symptoms of the bubonic plague. On the point of death, he wrote his *Devotions*. In Meditation 17 he expresses his faith in a God who would, beyond the death of death, make all things new and 'bind up all our scattered leaves again for that great library where every book shall lie open to one another.'

Donne was made better, not bitter, by his experience; 'I need thy thunder O my God,' he wrote. 'Thy music will not serve thee.'

After living on the point of death for many months, John Donne recovered and went on preaching God's good news.

5) *When we are hurting, God hurts with us – and then some.*

'Few give thought to the suffering that sin has caused our Creator . . . . As "the whole creation groans and travails in pain together" the heart of the infinite Father is pained in sympathy. Our world is a vast lazar house, a scene of misery that we dare not allow even our thoughts to dwell upon. Did we realize it as it is, the burden would be too terrible. *Yet God feels it all.*' *Education*, pages 263, 264.

In the midst of suffering, many feel let down by God. Why doesn't God get involved?

There *was* a time when God *did* intervene far more frequently than now. But what was the result? A generation witnessed the parting of the Red Sea, the daily gift of manna from heaven, the thunder from Sinai, and the pillar of smoke by day and of fire by night that indicated the close presence of God. But that generation lived in fear of God; and fear produced rebellion.

In after ages, the infinite God depended upon word of mouth through the prophets. That way people could listen, or not listen, as they chose.

Eventually, the sovereign God imprisoned Himself in human flesh and came personally to encounter and conquer suffering and death. He hung helplessly, the ultimate Victim, that He might be the ultimate Empathizer.

Jesus knows what it is to feel forsaken by man; His disciples fled from Gethsemane and were conspicuous by their absence from Calvary. He can even identify with those who feel forsaken by God; on the cross *He* felt forsaken. Hence His cry, 'My God, my God, why have you forsaken me?'

There is great meaning here.

In the beginning, God had given man freedom of choice but man had made wrong choices. Sin had blighted the planet and all who lived upon it. The focal facts of Christianity – an empty cross and an empty tomb – are indicators that the conquest of sin, suffering and death has been accomplished. Man has been given back his freedom to choose. With Christ as his

Calvary gave back to man his freedom to choose. With Christ as our Champion we can have pardon, peace and joy

Champion he can find pardon, peace, joy, assurance – and the *gift of trust*.

As we look to Jesus by faith, we see Him hurting with our hurt; see the Lamb slain in the funerals of our friends; slain in every victim of every catastrophe; slain in every vile deed and ugly word.

Does God care? Yes; and He cares enough to have done something about the evil in the world – at tremendous cost to Himself.

His Son's horrendous death ensured the eventual triumph of good over evil, of justice over injustice – and God's Good News Book assures us that Auschwitz, the evil empire behind it, and any and every other evil tyranny, great or small, shall be avenged, shall not rise up a second time – *and that there will be a great and glorious day of restoration.*

The bottom-line promise of God's Good News Book?

'Thy dead too shall live . . . .'

Is there life
after life?

Our school secretary was a woman we boys would willingly have named streets after. She was one very bright – and caring – lady. Which makes it all the harder to understand why she made the mistake which caused so much embarrassment to the headmaster and staff that ill-fated Christmas. Decades on, I incline to the theory that, under seasonal pressure, she had subcontracted out that particular piece of work to some unqualified person.

No Hell!

We were an Anglican school. It was our custom to make much of Christmas. Our carol service, remarkable for the lusty singing of the lads, took place in the Saxon church of St Peter. We sang the carols from a sheet typed up by the school secretary. But that particular Christmas service dissolved into raucous laughter during the first carol, 'The First Noel'. The refrain of the carol, customarily rendered, 'Noel, Noel', appeared on our sheets as 'No Hell! No Hell!'

We were sorry we had laughed so heartily when we learned that the secretary's Christmas present from the headmaster was a letter terminating her employment. To this day, that harsh action by our revered headmaster seems totally out of character.

Just, for that matter, as hell had always seemed, to my mind, to be totally out of character with God.

When the New Year arrived, the summary dismissal of our beloved school secretary was still an issue. And so was hell.

In our divinity classes, a conscientious attempt had been made to introduce us to the God who is the personification of love (1 John 4:8). But at the same time the reverend gentleman who taught us had also introduced us to the standard notions of popular theology, including the one that man was born with an 'immortal soul'; that death was a translation to another kind of life – saints in heaven, sinners in hell.

Cross-questioned about hell, our teacher went on to explain that it was a state of torture-by-fire that went on for ever and ever. It was, he said, not only for those who *did* the wrong things, but for those who *believed* the wrong things. Further, that the sufferings of those in hell – relatives, friends – were visible to those in heaven. Also visible to heaven's residents, he told us, were the doings of earthlings. . . .

There and then, the majority of my classmates abandoned God or Christianity or both; and a few resolved that if that was how God dealt with His enemies (and even His friends!), then their lives would be lived in defiance óf Him and all His ideals.

Is it possible that Hell is the foulest slander ever uttered against the character of God?

For myself, I decided that if hell was part of the picture, then the good news of Scripture was tainted by tyranny.

Is God a tyrant who burns His enemies eternally? Or is hell the foulest, most wicked slander ever uttered against the character of our all-loving Creator and Redeemer – devised by His arch-enemy, Satan?

The debate on Hell

In the years since I was a schoolboy, no doctrine of popular theology has been subjected to more close scrutiny than 'the immortality of the soul' and its corollary, an eternally burning hell.

When John Wenham wanted to publish *The Enigma of Evil*, it was hard for him to find a publisher. However, in 1974, IVP became the first evangelical publishing house to challenge the traditional doctrine of hell. Among those who were influenced by this book was the American evangelical Edward Fudge, who published *The Fire that Consumes* – foreword by F. F. Bruce – in 1982.

In 1988 arguably the greatest preacher-theologian of them all, John Stott, was challenged by liberal theologian David Edwards to state his view honestly on the punishment of the wicked. This Stott did in the book *Essentials*. Since Stott, hell has, as it were, drawn heavy fire.

'I want to repudiate with all the vehemence of which I am capable,' wrote John Stott, 'the glibness, what almost appears to be the glee, with which some evangelicals speak about hell . . . .'

The arguments of those who have abandoned 'the immortality of the soul' and 'hell' hinge on the meaning of *soul*, *spirit* and *body*.

Body, soul and spirit

So what, exactly, is a 'soul'?

When God told the first man and woman that the natural consequence of sin would be death (the deprivation of life), Satan decided to cast doubt on His truthfulness. The two lies with which he ensnared Adam and Eve were 'You will not die' (that is, death will not mean the deprivation of life) and 'You will be like God' (that is, immortal, deathless, indestructible). These primal lies have their echoes today in Spiritualism, Hinduism and Buddhism, as well as in the pseudo-Christian doctrine of 'the immortality of the soul'.

In Genesis 2:7 God, having created man, is described as making him a 'living soul' by breathing breath into his body. This suggests that body plus breath equals soul.

The conscientious scholars who have challenged 'the immortality of the soul' have searched both Old and New Testaments in vain for evidence of an immortal soul. In their search, they have uncovered verses like Ezekiel 18:4, 'The soul that sinneth, it shall die,' and Revelation 16:3, 'Every living soul died.' (KJV.) As they leafed through their Old Testaments, they found many references to 'souls' being 'cut off with the sword'.

In the end, facts had to be faced. The words translated 'soul' and 'spirit' occurred 1,642 times in the Bible and, further, that that represented 1,642 opportunities for an explanation that a 'soul' or 'spirit' can function consciously without a body. But not one text said that. There was not a single text that supported the view that 'soul' or 'spirit' or 'person' could be interpreted as an immaterial substance that functioned independently of a body. For this reason, the scholars have reached the conclusion that 'soul' or 'spirit' seems to refer to 'the energizing life-force given by God', *breath*, for short.

The silence of Lazarus

Let's learn a lesson from Lazarus.

Lazarus, it will be recalled, died. His story is in John 11. He didn't just lapse into a coma, and he wasn't on some life-support machine. He was as dead as a man could be. So dead, in fact, that they buried him. They put him in a cave and rolled a great stone in front of it, after carefully preparing his body and wrapping it in the grave-clothes customary at the time.

So it can be well and truly said that Lazarus was dead. But Jesus, his friend, came to the cemetery in Bethany and said, 'Lazarus, come out.' Lazarus 'came out'. Always the practical man, Jesus then gave orders that he should be freed from the grave-clothes and restored to his sisters. There was great rejoicing.

And here is where we learn an important lesson about death. Christians can accept the death of Lazarus, and, by faith, his resurrection. But over the centuries there is one thing they have found very difficult to understand: *the silence of Lazarus*.

According to popular theology the soul of Lazarus should, at the point of death, have been freed from his body and found lodgement in heaven or hell. Since Lazarus had been a man of faith, it has tended to be assumed that his

soul would have found
lodgement in heaven. For four days he was a corpse.

Before his resurrection, his sisters made it clear to Jesus that decay and
decomposition had already set in. His 'soul', therefore, should have quite
positively left for realms afar.

But Jesus came and called him back. Back from where? From the boulevards of paradise where he had been wandering with awe for four days? Had
that been the case, would not Lazarus have betrayed just a little impatience
at being snatched back to this vale of tears when he had had a sublime taste
of heaven? Why didn't he say, 'O Master, why didn't you leave me where I
was? Why did you recall me to this place where I must always endure pain
and sorrow and hardship – even though it is good to see my sisters again?'

And that is not the only mysterious thing for Christians about the silence
of Lazarus. Why didn't he then begin to tell of all the marvellous things he
had seen and experienced? To tell everyone, 'Don't get upset at the prospect
of death; heaven makes it worth while'?

No such ecstasy broke from the lips of the resurrected Lazarus; neither
were there any such recriminations for being deprived of the bliss that only
heaven can offer. Why the silence? A conspiracy of silence, perhaps? Was
Jesus party to this silence about what Lazarus saw when he was light years
away in heaven? Would Christ have brought Lazarus back to tread the dusty
roads of this sin-cursed planet if Lazarus had, in fact, been enjoying the
marvels of heaven?

Is it possible that the reason for the silence of Lazarus is that Lazarus saw nothing of heaven? That he wasn't travelling the golden streets or sitting at the feet of angels?

The nature of death

Before he went to raise Lazarus, Jesus told His disciples that Lazarus was sleeping (John 11:11-14). Is that significant? Is that what death is? A dreamless sleep, nothing more, nothing less? The sister of Lazarus didn't expect to see her brother until the resurrection day when all the righteous will be raised (verse 24). She said so. She didn't think for one moment that Lazarus was in paradise. She didn't imagine that some intangible 'soul' was wafting its triumphant flight through realms of glory. If she had imagined this, would she have wanted Lazarus to be brought back to life?

Was Lazarus silent about what happened in those four days for the simple reason that nothing happened to him in those four days? That his body simply began the process of returning to the dust from which mankind is created? That when he was restored to life, that process was halted and reversed as Christ restored to him the breath of life?

Jesus was always clear that death was a sleep. Referring to the dead daughter of Jairus, He said, ' "She is not dead, but sleeping." ' Luke 8:52, RSV. And in declaring death to be a dreamless sleep Christ was echoing words He had inspired the Old Testament seers to write centuries before. 'Lighten mine eyes,' the Psalmist had prayed, 'lest I sleep the sleep of death.' Psalm 13:3, KJV. Both Old and New Testaments call death a sleep – *sixty-one times*. In sound sleep there is no consciousness. In Psalm 146:3, 4 it is made very clear that when man's

The **problem** with **purgatory**

Bible translator William Tyndale declared to a Catholic opponent, 'Ye, in putting them [departed souls] in heaven, hell and purgatory, destroy the argument wherewith Christ and Paul prove the resurrection. . . . If the souls be in heaven, tell me why they be not in as good case as the angels be? And then what cause is there of the resurrection?' Tyndale's Preface to his New Testament, 1534 edition.

breath leaves his body, 'he returneth to his earth; in that very day his thoughts perish'. 'The dead praise not the Lord, neither any that go down into silence.' Psalm 115:17. 'For the living know that they shall die: but the dead know not anything. . . . Their love, and their hatred, and their envy, is now perished.' Ecclesiastes 9:5, 6. 'He that goeth down to the grave . . . shall return no more to his house, neither shall his place know him any more.' Job 7:9, 10. (All KJV.)

Martin Luther once stated: 'With very few exceptions, the dead sleep in utter insensibility till the day of judgement. . . . On what authority can it be said that the souls of the dead may not sleep out the interval between earth and heaven, or hell, or purgatory, in the same way that the living pass in profound slumber the interval between their down-lying at night and their uprising in the morning?' Michelet's *Life of Luther* (Bohn's edition), page 133.

Bible writers know nothing of the theory that the dead exist consciously in heaven or in hell prior to the resurrection. It was the breath given by God which first animated the faultless body of the first man and bestowed consciousness, and the testimony of the Bible is that death simply reverses the process.

In James 2:26 we read that 'the body without the spirit is dead'. In the margin we find that an alternative translation for *spirit* is 'breath'. 'The body without the breath is dead.' The spirit, or the breath, is what keeps the body alive.

Where did Hell come from?

As with Sunday observance, the notion of an ever-burning hell was absorbed into Roman Christianity from paganism.

So are there *no* Scriptures to support the idea of an ever-burning hell?

Jude 7 says that Sodom and Gomorrah were destroyed by 'eternal fire'. If that's part of the evidence for hell, it's not very convincing. The Dead Sea now covers the site of the cities of the plain. 'Eternal fire' was eternal in only one sense: *its effect*.

Malachi 4:1 speaks of evildoers being burned like chaff. How does chaff burn? Just a puff, and it's gone. (NEB.)

In Matthew 25:41, speaking of the irredeemably wicked, Jesus said: 'Then shall he say unto them on his left hand, Depart from me, ye cursed, into everlasting fire.' (KJV.) But reference to the Greek text leaves us in this, as in every other instance, in the opposite direction from the idea of an ever-lasting holocaust. Instead, there is the idea that the *results* of the fire of judgement are everlasting.

Who invented the idea of an ever-burning Hell?
Only the *results* of the fires of judgement are everlasting

Eternal death is not a painful form of eternal life.

The most vivid picture of hell – not contained in the *Codex Sinaiticus* – contains the words 'Where their worm dieth not, and the fire is not quenched' (Mark 9:48, KJV). This is a quotation from Isaiah 66:24 where the dead bodies of God's enemies are consigned to the city's rubbish dump to be eaten by maggots and burned. John Stott insists that Jesus' use of Isaiah 66:24 does not mention everlasting pain. What He says is that the worm will not die and the fire will not be quenched – until, presumably, their work of destruction is done.

The book of Revelation refers to a 'lake of fire' in which all who have finally rejected God will be cast (20:14). But Stott insists this is the language of destruction; the imagery of fire indicates instantaneous annihilation, not everlasting punishment.

'We wish you not to remain in ignorance, brothers, about those who sleep

A **promise** to a **thief**

Supporters of the belief that, at death, man goes immediately to either heaven or hell have cited the promise of Jesus to the thief on the cross, recorded in Luke 23:43.

The New Testament was written in Greek – and there was no punctuation. The meaning of this promise depends upon the placing of a comma! Punctuation was added to the New Testament by translators.

The meaning of the verse depends entirely on whether the comma is in death,' wrote Paul the apostle. And with good reason; for on this all-important question turns also the significance of *life*. Paul continues: 'You should not grieve like the rest of men, who have no hope. We believe that Jesus died and rose again; and so it will be for those who died as Christians; God will bring them to life with Jesus. For this we tell you as the Lord's word: we who are left alive until the Lord comes shall not forestall those who have died; because at the word of command, at the sound of the archangel's voice and God's trumpet call, the Lord himself will descend from heaven; first the Christian dead will rise, then we who are left alive shall join them, caught up in clouds to meet the Lord in the air. Thus we shall always be with the Lord.' 1 Thessalonians 4:13-18, NEB.

At last, then, the really good news about death. Though it may run the most robust of us down, it need hold no terrors. Man is born, lives, grows and may pass away, but he has roots among eternal things.

placed before or after the word *today*. It has been placed before; it should have been placed after.

Jesus was saying, '*Today*, when my own disciples have forsaken me. *Today*, when my own people have crucified me. *Today*, when it appears that I shall never have a kingdom. *Today*, when it looks as though I shall never save anybody. I say unto you today, You will be with me in paradise.'

Death, for the Son of God, was to be like that which comes to every man – quiet, restful sleep. He was to be resurrected, not from three days in paradise, but from three days in the tomb. He said to Mary when He made Himself known on that Sunday morning, ' "Do not hold on to me, for I have not yet returned to the Father." ' John 20:17.

The crucified thief looked far past that dark hour when he said, 'Remember me when thou comest into thy kingdom.' He looked far down the corridors of time to the day when He whose right it is to reign shall receive the kingdom from His Father. And Jesus, cheered by his faith, responded, 'I say unto you today, You will be with me in paradise.'

There is life after death

The resurrection of Jesus ensured the death of death. And on the strong and sufficient evidence of an empty tomb in an Easter garden, and of a risen Lord walking and talking and eating with men along evening roads of sadness to wide boulevards of joy, is based the good news of an ever-open future. That, though a man dies – if he believes in Jesus – he has a title to eternity and will rise again – because Jesus rose again.

But before that 'life everlasting' the Lord Himself must descend from heaven to awaken the saints who sleep in death. And, because God neither forces Himself nor His salvation on anyone, there is the option to reject both Him and His offer – an offer not backed up by the threat of an ever-burning hell. Thank God! The good news does not have behind it the taint of tyranny! 'No Hell! No Hell!': not a bad message after all.

'I am the Resurrection and the Life,' said Jesus. 'He that believeth on me, though he were dead yet shall he live.' So man's immortality is not innate, or natural. It is *conditional*. That is why the Bible's greatest verse says, 'Whosoever believes in me shall not perish but have everlasting life.' John 3:16. When Jesus Christ returns, and not before, 'this mortal must put on immortality. So when this corruptible shall have put on incorruption, and this mortal shall have put on immortality, then shall be brought to pass the saying that is written, Death is swallowed up in victory. O death, where is thy sting? O grave, where is thy victory?' 1 Corinthians 15:53-56, KJV.

The poet-preacher John Donne, centuries ago, had it right as he stared into the face of death with the light of victory already shining in his eyes; 'Death be not proud, though some have called thee mighty and dreadful, for thou art not so. . . . One short sleep past, we wake eternally, and death shall be no more; death *thou* shalt die.'

God's Good News

Future tense

Sirens wail over frightened cities.
Nerves are taut like piano wire.

Now what? Another air attack? Or a bomb explosion?

We live in the age of the terrorist. We live on edge; beyond the edge is a precipice; we live from moment to nail-biting moment. The future grows dark under menacing thunderheads: the dust clouds of advancing armies, the spectre-shroud of famine, the acrid stench of polluted air, the mushroom cloud of mega-death.

Future tense.

Tense as a wire about to snap.

Nerves, taut as piano wire – ready to snap

The future industry

Having taken the pulse of our hope-scarce times, thousands have rushed into the pseudo-science, 'futurology'. For the age of terror is also the age of *un*reason. To get at the future, people peer at crystals, crystal balls, astrology charts. The whole ghoulish bag of tricks – seances, channelling sessions, black magic, white magic, New Age – is back in fashion.

Seventy-eight per cent of Americans consult, on a regular basis, an astrologer, a New Age channeller, or predictive data assembled by astrologers and channellers. Every British national newspaper carries a 'Your Future in the Stars' column; the top people's paper, *The Times*, giving disproportionate space to astrological features.

The future is big business. And frightened people, insecure about life and livelihood, are gullible people.

The best-known Hollywood moguls, producers, actors and actresses are into New Age to varying degrees. Media astrologers and New Age gurus command among the highest incomes in our societies.

Living with a nightmarish present, to shut out the thunder from the future, millions rush madly into the death-embrace of instant pleasure, thrusting their heads into the silver-screen. The best-known people in the world are those to whom we pay huge salaries to take our minds off reality.

And, sadly, the urgent need of the masses to know the future has led many to turn to religious cranks who use the Bible in the same way that the psychic uses a crystal ball. They come up with astonishing calculations that prove that Armageddon is due the day after tomorrow. And when it doesn't happen? The cranks are nowhere to be found. But, in the perception of the people, God's Good News Book has in some way been devalued.

Secular doom howlers

Some scientists and scholars predict the end of the world. How do they say it will happen?

✪ **Anarchy** – the breakdown of societies through unstoppable law-lessness.

Earth warming, pollution and climate changes lead to mega famines, even anarchy

○ **Climate changes** – causing weather-related, mega-disasters and, ultimately, a planet hostile to human life.

○ **Disease** – the raft of 'new', drug-resistant diseases that threaten the human species: the ebola virus, AIDS. The return of the drug-resistant 'old' diseases: TB, malaria, cholera, diphtheria.

○ **Drought** – as populations and deserts expand, wetlands vanish and lakes, seas and rivers shrink.

○ **Famine** – a seventh (800 million) of our world's population is already chronically undernourished. Worldwatch Institute, based on shifts in the world's food economy, predicts that 'from a long-accustomed period of overall abundance we are entering a period of scarcity – and we cannot see beyond it'.

○ **Over-population.**

○ **Pollution** – the prospect of Total Toxic Overload: an uninhabitable planet.

○ **A new-style nuclear menace** – with the end of the Cold War and the emergence of a one super-power world, diplomats negotiate nuclear disarmament.

But the republics of the one-time Soviet Union are chronically unstable, economically and politically. Organized crime defies government. And one of the world's biggest nuclear arsenals is sold off, item by item. . . .

Suddenly the prospect of sophisticated, international terrorist organizations able to hold the planet to ransom comes out of the realm of fiction, into that of real probability. Suddenly there is talk of 'Islam's bomb' and, with the apparently unstoppable spread of Islamic fundamentalism, the prospect of nuclear power in the hands of ayatollahs.

There is good news

History *is* shifting its gears. The pace *is* increasing. Man's hand is on the steering wheel. But the vehicle, though heading for a smash-up, is not totally out of control. Behind all is the Hand of an all-powerful God who will intervene right on cue.

The instant Bible expositors who have treated God's book like a crystal ball and, in consequence, brought it into disrepute with many thinking people, are marching to the devil's drumbeat. Satan wants you to laugh off Bible prophecies just at the time when they are all being fulfilled and history is reaching its prophesied climax.

God's Good News Book is the only source of hope for the future. Bible prophecies which foretell the future course of history with incredible accuracy *have* to have something in them for us. We should be at liberty to disbelieve them, except that most of them have been fulfilled already – and can easily be authenticated from history. The prophecies project us into our own day and – Daniel taken together with Jesus, Paul, Peter and John in the New Testament – describe the very conditions prevailing in the world right now.

Only the climax is missing, has yet to be fulfilled.

Tyre was once a proud, boastful city on the Levantine coast, north of Palestine. The city was, its inhabitants believed, totally invincible. Even if the mainland city were to be captured, they could always retire to their stronghold on an offshore island. In 590BC, the prophet Ezekiel had spoken for God: ' "I am against you, O Tyre, and I will bring many nations against you, like the sea casting up its waves. They will destroy the walls of Tyre and pull down her towers; I will scrape away her rubble and make her a bare rock. Out in the sea she will become a place to spread fishing nets, for I have spoken, declares the sovereign Lord. She will become plunder for the nations."' Ezekiel 26:3-5.

The siege of Tyre began almost immediately. After thirteen years the 'invincible' port city was left in smouldering ruins. But what about the off-shore island? Could it ever become a bare rock, a place for the spreading of nets? This prophecy was not fulfilled for another 250 years. Alexander the Great captured this hostile, boastful island city and made of it the same kind of ruin as the port city. He captured it by using the rubble of old Tyre to build a causeway through the sea to the island.

Similarly, at a time when the fall of Babylon was impossible to conceive, God, through Isaiah (13:19-21), prophesied, in considerable detail, that city's total destruction. Every detail was subsequently fulfilled.

The birth, ministry, death and resurrection of Jesus were prophesied in detail in the Old Testament.

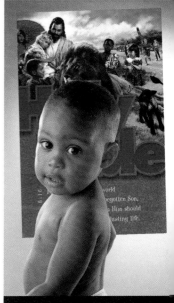

God's book is *the* book of good news for the future

Old Testament Daniel saw a panorama of history from the time of the Babylonian Empire to the establishment on earth of God's eternal kingdom.

What Old Testament Daniel saw, New Testament Peter saw – and described in even more vivid detail. 'The day of the Lord will come as suddenly and unexpectedly as a thief. In that day the heavens will disappear in a terrific, tearing blast, the very elements will disintegrate in heat and the earth and all that is in it will be burnt up to nothing. In view of the fact that all these things are to be dissolved, what sort of people ought you to be? . . . True, this day will mean that the heavens will disappear in fire and the elements disintegrate in fearful heat, but our hopes are set not on these but on the new Heavens and the new earth which he has promised us, and in which nothing but good shall live.' 2 Peter 3:10-13, Phillips.

Did the apostle John preview the same holocaust and attempt to describe it? 'There was a tremendous earthquake, the sun turned dark like coarse black cloth, and the full moon was red as blood. The stars of the sky fell upon the earth, just as a fig tree sheds unripe figs when shaken in a gale. The sky vanished as though it were a scroll being rolled up, and every mountain and island was jolted out of its place.' Revelation 6:12-14, Phillips.

Future tense?

Sounds like future tense, yes? Not at all. Future perfect!

Prophecy is not about frightening pictures of the future. Indeed, it is not primarily about the future. It's about the *now*. It's about understanding that, no matter how things may look to you at the moment, God is in control; His purposes and plans will triumph (Isaiah 46:9, 10). And, most of all, prophecy is about saying 'Yes' to God's great offer of forgiveness through Calvary – and new life through new birth.

On the night before His crucifixion, Jesus, for the benefit of His followers in all ages, said, 'There's no need for fear! No need for stress! I'm going away to prepare a place for you in my Father's house. And I shall most certainly return to take you home that we may be together for ever.' (See John 14:1-3.)

With that in mind, let's take a look at Daniel's great panorama of the future.

After Daniel, we'll take a look at what Jesus Himself and, later, Paul said about the signs that would indicate that the return of Jesus was near.

And, finally, we shall examine how, from the Mission Control of the universe, God gave the apostle John a colourful picture of an end-time crisis in the book of Revelation.

'I've heard that's a *terrifying* book,' somebody complains.

Not so. It was written to ensure that the future for God's friends would *not* be terrifying. Written as a revelation of Jesus Christ. Written to charge God's friends to preach His good news about Jesus with greater urgency. Written to bring the fence-straddlers down on to God's side before it's too late.

Prophecy *is* a sneak preview of human history, yes. But, more than that, God intended it as a light from heaven to illuminate the way through this dark world to the next (2 Peter 1:19).

The **Last Empire**

Some things don't change. Back in Babylon – the golden Empire at the height of its power under Nebuchadnezzar – a Bible prophet had to fight for his place among the horoscope-pedlars and the psychics. It was among the pagan superstitions of Babylon that the whole kit and caboodle – from astrology to astral projection – that we now dignify with the label 'New Age' had its heyday. But, contrary to popular assertion, it did not originate there. Several centuries earlier, God had told the Hebrews that fortune-tellers, astrologers, magicians and clairvoyants were 'an abomination unto the Lord' (Deut. 18:9-12, KJV).

Why was God so hard on the psychics? Because a practitioner of the occult, then, as now, was openly giving allegiance to the enemy of man and God: Satan.

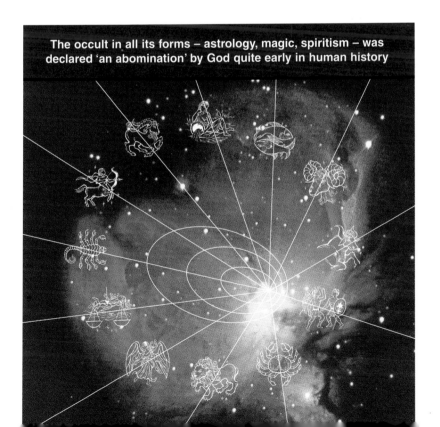

The occult in all its forms – astrology, magic, spiritism – was declared 'an abomination' by God quite early in human history

So is God deliberately trying to keep us in the dark about the future? Not at all. 'The Sovereign Lord does nothing without revealing his plan to his servants the prophets.' Amos 3:7.

To His servants the psychics? No. His servants the prophets. And how does God communicate with the prophets? 'When a prophet of the Lord is among you, I reveal myself to him in visions, I speak to him in dreams.' Numbers 12:6.

Visions and dreams – given to prophets. Not mutterings to mediums. Not through crystal balls or horoscope charts. For reasons discussed in the last chapter, God wants us to have a sneak preview of the future. And He wants us to get it straight.

A forgotten dream

Among the most brilliant intellects at the court of Nebuchadnezzar, King of Babylon, was a Hebrew captive – Daniel. Among the conquests of the Golden Empire had been Daniel's homeland, west of the Jordan. And Nebuchadnezzar, by contrast to some modern politicians who prefer the mutterings of mediums to the predictions of prophets, had made sure that the cream of the intelligentsia of the countries he conquered became part of his government and the political infrastructure of his empire.

But Nebuchadnezzar hedged his bets. His court was thronged with astrologers when Daniel and his friends arrived. And Daniel the prophet had to establish the reputation not only of himself but of his God.

Check out the story in Daniel chapter 2. One night King Nebuchadnezzar had a dream. Since it was God who gave it to him, we may also assume that it was God who caused him to forget it. But the king hung on to one thing when he woke up: the forgotten dream had contained something of the

utmost importance.

Nebuchadnezzar summoned all the astrologers, the psychics and the magicians into the throne room:

' "I have had a dream that troubles me and I want to know what it means." ' Verse 3.

The assortment of psychics panicked. Give them a dream, and they could always invent some sort of interpretation. But their Satan-source had little idea what the future held; and no idea at all what the king had dreamt..

Those were the days of absolute monarchs on whose lightest whim hung everyone's life. Nebuchadnezzar told the astrologers that unless they could, first, tell him what he had dreamt, and, second, interpret what he had dreamt, he would make mincemeat of them – *literally* (Verse 5)! If, by contrast, they could describe and interpret the dream – there would be honours and gifts without measure.

The psychics played for time; 'If the king would only *tell* us what he has dreamt . . .' But the king was ahead of the game; ' "I am certain that you are trying to gain time, . . ." ' Verse 8. And he repeated his conditions. There was an edge of fierce determination in his voice.

What *could* the Satan-servers do? This time they protested: ' "There is not a man on earth who can do what the king asks! No king, however great and mighty, has ever asked such a thing of any magician or enchanter or astrologer. What the king asks is too difficult. No one can reveal it to the king except the gods, and they do not live among men." ' Verses 10, 11.

The king's fury knew no bounds. He gave an order for the execution of all his advisers; and that included Daniel and his Hebrew friends, as well as the psychics.

Daniel had already established a reputation for courtesy, wisdom and tact – even among the king's guards. He was able to ask the commander of the guard why the king had issued such a harsh decree. Soon Daniel was abreast of the events of the morning.

A panorama of history

Daniel requested an audience with the king. He asked for time to interpret the dream; and Nebuchadnezzar must have seen something in his

Interpretation of Nebuchadnezzar's dream

Head of Gold
Babylon
605-539 BC

Chest of Silver
Medo-Persia
539-331 BC

Thighs of Bronze
Greece
331-168 BC

Legs of Iron
Rome
168 BC-AD 476

Feet of Iron and Clay
Divided Europe
AD 476-Second
Advent

manner to give him confidence. Extra time was granted. With three other Hebrews, Daniel returned to his house. According to established habit, they shared quality time with God, praying for His guidance.

That night Daniel had a vision. He saw an outline panorama of the future down to the end of time. He saw, too, that behind the play and counter-play of history's political posturers, the agencies of the all-merciful God silently, patiently, worked out the counsels of His own will (verses 17-23).

The following morning found Daniel, in company with the commander of the guard, in Nebuchadnezzar's audience chamber.

'Are you able to tell me what I saw in my dream and interpret it?' asked the king.

Daniel's reply is worth noting; ' "No wise man, enchanter, magician or diviner can explain to the king the mystery he has asked about, but there is a God in heaven who reveals mysteries. He has shown King Nebuchadnezzar what will happen in days to come. Your dream and the visions that passed through your mind as you lay on your bed are these . . . ." '

And, in the court of the world's mightiest ruler, you could have heard a pin drop.

Concern for the future had, said Daniel, preoccupied the king as he had fallen asleep. God, the great Revealer of mysteries, had chosen to give the Babylonian emperor – for our benefit as well as for his – an overview of the future to the end of time.

In vision the king had seen ' "a large statue – an enormous, dazzling statue, awesome in appearance" '.

The king's eyes widened. Yes, that was it!

He listened breathlessly as Daniel described the statue:

Its head was of gold.

Its chest and arms were of silver.

Its thighs were of bronze.

Its legs were of iron.

Its feet – part iron, part clay.

Daniel's description checked perfectly with what the king had seen. But there had been something else. What *had* it been?

Yes! A vast boulder 'cut out, but not by human hands' struck the statue on its feet – and smashed them. In seconds the entire edifice was reduced to powder blowing in the wind. And the wind swept all trace of the image away. Then 'the rock that struck the statue became a huge mountain and filled the whole earth.' Verse 35.

The interpretation

' "You",' Daniel said simply, ' "are the head of gold . . . ." ' And Nebuchadnezzar's head tilted back; the corners of his mouth rose and it was as if his eyes peered proudly down the arches of the future.

But his eyes refocused on Daniel as he heard him say, ' "After you, another kingdom will rise, inferior to yours . . . ." ' This young prophet was no aspiring politician, Nebuchadnezzar decided. His temporary fantasy of a mighty empire that would last until the end of time was blasted. And he was not well pleased. His short-lived empire would be swept away – by an inferior power. And that rankled with the king. At a later time he would construct a great statue *all* of gold. He would set it on the Plain of Dura – and command everybody to worship it or burn!

Daniel continued. ' "Next, a third kingdom, one of bronze, will rule over the whole earth . . . ." ' By then Nebuchadnezzar knew that the young man before him was not giving him political advice on the lines of, 'Don't go out tomorrow – your stars are wrong'. He was receiving from him, and his God, a privileged preview of the mighty sweep of history.

How it all happened

And it all panned out as per prediction.

Daniel was still at the Babylonian court when Cyrus entered the Golden City in 539BC, thus establishing the second world empire. The circumstances were dramatic. The feast of Belshazzar, and the bloodless hand writing the epitaph of an empire on the wall as the courtiers revelled.

The Medes and the Persians represented the two silver arms of the statue. Medo-Persia was the dominant empire until, in 331BC, Alexander the Great, the bringer of the bronze kingdom, established Greek-Macedon power from the Balkans to the northern mountains of India.

But the empire of brass would be replaced by the empire of iron: Rome. And Rome's power would last from 168BC to AD476.

What then?

A divided continent

Daniel was drawing to a conclusion. He had reached the feet of the statue; ten toes representing ten kingdoms (see Daniel 7:24). And those ten kingdoms, the modern nations of Europe, would never again be reunited permanently under one government. In Daniel's words, ' "And just as you saw the iron mixed with baked clay, so the people will be a mixture and will not remain united, any more than iron mixes with clay." ' Verse 43.

That was a long shot! What God, through Daniel, was telling Nebuchadnezzar is not without interest to us. After the fall of Rome, Europe would never again be united.

How has that prediction worked out?

Thus far, the prophecy of Daniel 2, reaching up to the present, has been fulfilled to the letter.

Charlemagne attempted to unite the divided nations of Europe but failed.

Holy Roman Emperor Charles V attempted to do the same, with the same end result.

Louis XIV of France tried and failed.

For many years Napoleon seemed to be succeeding but, after Waterloo in 1815, he said, 'God Almighty has been too much for me.'

In the twentieth century there was at least one crazed dictator who had the same vision. Hitler built the biggest empire of them all; at the end of 1942 he controlled an empire that stretched from Stalingrad to the Channel coast. His was 'the thousand-year Reich'. Now his delusions of grandeur stand out for what they were: the products of a diseased mind.

Political conditions in Europe at the moment are, we are told, particularly favourable towards federal union. Somewhat prematurely the term

'European union' is already in use. Politicians in many major European countries favour such a union. But there is a power vacuum at the centre. Who will endeavour to fill it? And for how long will they succeed?

As we watch events unfold, let us keep in mind the last, and by far the most exciting part of Daniel's interpretation of the king's vision. In *this* age of division a ' "rock cut out of the mountain, but not by human hands" ' (verse 45), would be hurled at the feet of the image and smash it to pieces. ' "And in the days of those kings the God of heaven will set up a kingdom which will never be destroyed, and that kingdom will not be left for another people; it will crush and put an end to all these kingdoms, but it will itself endure for ever." ' Verse 44, NASB.

The idea of a united Europe has been around for some time. Bible prophecy indicates that it will not succeed

In the days of those kings – the nations of modern Europe – God Himself will gatecrash human history.

The problems of the world – pollution, wars, terrorism, political tensions – are beyond solution. Neither politicians nor scientists have the answers. *The solution to the world's problems will be a supernatural one.* The only hope for the world is an encounter with Jesus – of a close and final kind – when He returns to the earth in splendour.

His will be the Final Empire.

It will be recalled that, thus far, the prophecy has been fulfilled to the letter. It would be reckless in the extreme to believe with the materialists, the psychics and the astrologers that this tired old world will go on for ever. The books of Daniel and the Revelation, the prophecies of Jesus, of Paul, of John and of Peter, are closely tied together. They were written for our day. They draw back the curtain of the future.

And, dazzling that future: the arrival of the Final Empire.

The **crisis**
of the **antichrist**

Given God's foreknowledge, would it not be reasonable to assume that He would forewarn His people, through His prophets, of the plans of the enemy? To warn of bad news to ensure the final fulfilment of the good? After all, forewarned is forearmed. Yes?

Decoding prophecy

The key books of Bible prophecy are Daniel and the Revelation. To these must be added the prophetic passages in the teaching of Jesus (Matt. 24; Mark 13; Luke 21), and of Paul (1 Thess. 4:13-18; 2 Thess. 2), and of Peter (2 Peter 2, 3) and prophetic warnings from John outside his book of Revelation (1 John 2:18-27; 4:1-6).

The prophetic books and passages are all interrelated.

In prophetic books and passages God uses picture language from time to time. For example, animals or 'beasts' are used to represent nations. A woman is used to represent a church; a beautiful woman representing God's true church (Jer. 6:2 and Rev. 12:1-5), and a corrupt woman representing a false church (Revelation 17:3-5). But God has not set out to confuse us! What would be the point? His prophetic symbols are consistent, whether they are in the Old Testament or the New.

So why use symbols at all? In giving His people a preview of history, God found it necessary to trace the future activities of political and religious powers hostile to Him and to His people. To name names would have been to invite the destruction of the Book by its enemies.

Both Daniel and Revelation foretell a time of persecution for God's people. So important is this time period that it is mentioned seven times. Here God *really* descended into detail. He gave His prophets *time* prophecies. To decode these time prophecies it is vital to understand that God uses a day to represent a literal year.

The Year-Day Principle is *implicit*, rather than *explicit* in Scripture. Sir Isaac Newton, a great student of prophecy as well as a great scientist, stated confidently: 'Daniel's days are years.' (Sir Isaac Newton, *Observations upon*

THE SEVENTY WEEKS PROPHECY OF **DANIEL 9:23-27**

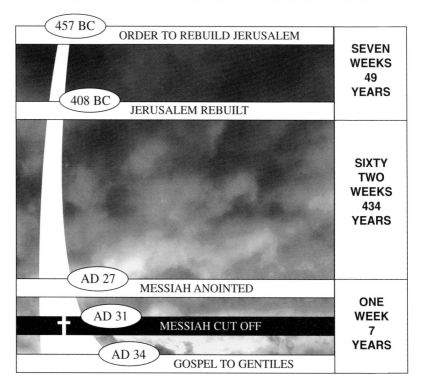

457 BC — ORDER TO REBUILD JERUSALEM	**SEVEN WEEKS 49 YEARS**
408 BC — JERUSALEM REBUILT	
	SIXTY TWO WEEKS 434 YEARS
AD 27 — MESSIAH ANOINTED	**ONE WEEK 7 YEARS**
AD 31 — MESSIAH CUT OFF	
AD 34 — GOSPEL TO GENTILES	

the Prophecies of Daniel and the Apocalypse of St John, page 122.) At least fourteen Jewish authors and 200 non-Jewish authors have applied the Year-Day Principle to time prophecy.

The one fail-safe proof of the Year-Day Principle is in the accuracy with which Daniel prophesied, hundreds of years in advance of the event, the anointing and crucifixion of Jesus:

'Seventy weeks [of years, or 490 years] are decreed upon your people and upon your holy city [Jerusalem], . . . Know therefore and understand that from the going forth of the commandment to restore and rebuild Jerusalem until [the coming of] the Anointed One, a Prince, shall be seven weeks [of years] and sixty-two weeks [of years]; . . . And after the sixty-two weeks [of years] shall the Anointed One be cut off or killed. . . . And he shall enter into a strong and firm covenant with the many for one week [seven years]. And in the midst of the week he shall cause the sacrifice and offering to cease.' Daniel 9:23-27, *The Amplified Bible.*

Seventy prophetic weeks represent 490 years. The time period begins at the time of the decree to rebuild Jerusalem. There were three of these issued by Persian kings but the final and complete decree was issued in the autumn of 457BC.

Sixty-nine of the seventy prophetic weeks (483 years) reached to Messiah. Beginning at 457BC, 483 years brings us to AD27 – the very year of Jesus' baptism and anointing with the Holy Spirit. The word 'Messiah' means 'the Anointed One'.

Luke, the careful historian, records Jesus' baptism as having taken place in the fifteenth year of the reign of Tiberius (Luke 3:1, 2); hence the accuracy with which we can pinpoint the date of the baptism.

It would appear that Jesus was familiar with the Year-Day Principle. He began His preaching with the words, 'The time is fulfilled.' Mark 1:15, KJV.

The last, or seventieth, week of the prophecy still remains. In the *middle* of that week, Messiah was to be 'cut off'. The ministry of Jesus was limited to three-and-a-half years from His baptism in the autumn of AD27 to the spring of AD31 when He was crucified.

What of the remaining three-and-a-half years allotted to confirm the covenant with Israel? Jesus' ministry was primarily to Israel; and after His resurrection His followers continued that ministry until the stoning of Stephen in AD34, when persecution scattered the disciples from Jerusalem. Acts 8:1-4. From that time, the Gospel was taken to the Gentiles.

Thus it is in application that we find the proof of the Year-Day Principle and, therefore, the main tool for the decoding of Bible prophecy.

Why did the death of Jesus 'in the midst of the week' 'cause the sacrifice and offering to cease'? Jesus died at 3pm on Good Friday or, in Jewish terms, the day of the Passover. Ever since the Exodus from Egypt nearly 1,500 years previously, each family in Israel had slain a lamb without blemish at the spring full-moon Passover festival. On that memorable Good Friday, the symbolism was precisely fulfilled. Jesus died at the ninth hour,

3pm, the hour for the Lamb to be slain. Hence Daniel's prophecy was accurate, not just to the year, or the half year, but to the day and the hour.

The time of persecution

Remember the 'time of persecution' that was prophesied seven times in Scripture? Daniel had it in chapter 7, verse 25, and chapter 12, verse 7. In Revelation it is found in chapter 12, verses 6 and 14, and chapter 13, verse 5 (see also Rev. 11: 2, 3).

Daniel's time period of 'a time, two times, and half a time' (RSV) was understood by John the Revelator as a year, two years, and half a year. Hence in Revelation 12:6 he wrote of 'a thousand two hundred and threescore days'. (KJV.) In other words: 1,260 years.

The Great **Apostasy**

In His Olivet sermon Jesus drew the attention of His followers to Daniel's prophecies (Matt. 24:15). Along with Daniel and Paul and John, Jesus foresaw the rise of counterfeit Christianity (Matt. 24:11, 21, 22).

The counterfeit Christianity, apostasy, and the antichrist prophesied by Jesus, Paul and John, came into being following the 'conversion' of Constantine. 'Official' Christianity became a mix of pagan and pious practice.

Into the vacuum left by the fall of the Roman Empire stepped the Bishop of Rome. From small beginnings (Daniel 7:8), a part political, part religious despotism developed which was confirmed by Justinian's decree of 538. This power was used to control and humiliate kings (7:20). There are countless examples of the papal power's speaking 'words against the most High' (7:25, KJV). At the Fifth Lateran Council (1512) it was declared concerning

Daniel had led up to this time prophecy by a repeat, in chapter 7, of the historical 'parade of the empires' he had already described in chapter 2.

This time, each empire was represented by a 'beast'. Babylon became a lion; Medo-Persia a bear; Greece a leopard; and Rome a terrifying beast with ten horns. But in Daniel 7 there is an added detail.

At the time of Rome's fall a power – represented by 'a little horn' (Dan. 7:8) – would emerge, arrogant and hostile to God's true followers. This power would menace God's people for much of the time period between the fall of imperial Rome and the establishment of God's kingdom at the end of time.

It was John who used the term 'antichrist' (1 John 2:18-23). It was this 'little horn' or 'antichrist' power that would be used by Satan to menace

the Pope: 'Thou art another God on earth.' In 1870, urged by Pope Pius IX, Council I issued a decree to the effect that a pontiff 'is infallible when he defines the truth'. (Anne Freemantle, *The Papal Encyclicals*, page 27.) It is unlikely that any power on earth has been responsible for more persecution than the Roman Catholic Church (7:25).

The Canons of Orleans were used to wipe out the Albigenses. The cruel office of the Inquisition was used against enemies of both Church and State. Hideously cruel attempts were made to extinguish the Waldenses. Countless Lollards were burned, as were Huss and Jerome and multitudes of their followers. Ferocious cruelties were practised in the Netherlands. In France, the Massacre of St Bartholomew's Eve was only one of many blood-lettings against the Huguenots in a persecution that would last well over a century.

But the Church of Rome does not hold a monopoly on intolerance. . . .

The good news of Christ's Gospel does not permit us to hate any man, woman or child for any reason. We should not lose sight of the fact that the papacy has held the allegiance of great saints of God in every age, including our own.

God's people and His plans for 1,260 years.

Antichrist exposed

We catch up with the antichrist power again at the beginning of Revelation 13. In the first two verses of this chapter this power with 'a blasphemous name' is associated with each of the four beasts typifying the ancient empires of Daniel 2 and 7: Babylon, Persia, Greece, Rome. It is associated with them all, because it sums them all up. How? These heathen empires had one thing in common: sun worship.

To appease the endless appetite of sun deities, rather than accept the Creator's gift of salvation, the heathen religions under these empires had burned babies, degraded women and engaged in all manner of barbarous practices.

Christians of the first century suffered hideous persecution for refusing to engage in any aspect of sun worship. Thousands were thrown to the lions or burned alive.

But, insidiously, ceremonies that mingled sun worship with Christian practice infiltrated the Church. When, in AD135, Emperor Hadrian outlawed Jewish worship, particularly the seventh-day Sabbath-keeping, Christians began to distance themselves from their Hebrew heritage. Between that time and Constantine's declaration in 321 of Christianity as the official religion of the Roman Empire, worship on the day of the sun replaced seventh-day Sabbath worship in many parts of the empire. Constantine's decree of 7 March 321 required all Christians to reverence the 'venerable day of the sun'. Anyone found worshipping on the seventh-day Sabbath could expect severe retribution.

In the centuries that followed, the use of fire and sword to enforce the mix of paganism and counterfeit Christianity became common. And those taking the brunt of this persecution were, invariably, the tiny minorities who held fast to Bible-based Christianity.

In Daniel 7:8, the 'little horn' with ' "eyes like the eyes of a man and a mouth that spoke boastfully" ' uprooted three of the ten horns on the head of the terrifying beast that represented Imperial Rome. By AD538 the Emperor Justinian had destroyed the last of the three tribes – the Heruli, the Vandals,

Pagan Rome persecuted Christians for refusing to engage in sun worship. The so-called 'Christian empire', after Constantine enforced Sunday worship on Christians

and the Ostrogoths – on behalf of counterfeit Christianity. The Western Empire was, from this time, dominated by the Roman Church and its bishop who, in power, effectively replaced the Roman emperor.

Paul had prophesied that, after a 'falling away', the 'man of sin' would take centre stage (2 Thessalonians 2:3, KJV). Examine the meaning of *antichrist. Anti* means 'against' or 'instead of' – either openly opposed to Christ or subtly overshadowing Him. 'I beheld', wrote Daniel, 'and the same [little] horn made war with the saints, and prevailed against them; . . .' (7:21, KJV.) Daniel continued; 'He shall speak great words against the most High, and shall wear out the saints of the most High, and shall think to change times and laws' – including the Sabbath commandment – for the 1,260 years of his domination (7:25).

Church reformers from Wyclif through to Luther, John Knox and Sir

Isaac Newton were emphatic in identifying 'antichrist', 'the little horn' and 'the man of sin' with the papacy. The 1,260 years of counterfeit Christian Church-and-State authority began with Justinian's decree of 538, following his defeat of the Ostrogoths. But at the times when they lived it was impossible to see what would bring to an end this long period of domination.

A deadly wound

In Revelation 13:3 it was prophesied that the long period of domination of the power typified as 'the beast' or 'antichrist' would end with a 'deadly wound'. Newton was one among many who had projected the 1,260-year prophecy to 1798. It is way past coincidence that in 1798 General Berthier, on behalf of the government of revolutionary France, captured the Pope, thus bringing to an end a dominance which had been confirmed by Justinian's decree just 1,260 years previously.

But here it is important that we pause for thought.

The institution, the lamentable record of which is laid bare in Scripture, is that of the papacy. *But Bible prophecy says not a word against individual Roman Catholics.* The institution anathematized by prophecy and by history has held the allegiance of some of the great saints of God, a few in our own day. The Holy Spirit works on the hearts of *all* men and women. Many members of the Roman Catholic communion have been and are devout and sincere. To say this is to state the obvious. The Roman Catholic Church does not have a monopoly on intolerance; anyone, any church, can partake of the spirit of antichrist.

Daniel was told that the apostate power would cast truth to the ground, that his heart would be 'set against the holy covenant' and that he would 'take action against it' and would 'take away the continual burnt offering' (Dan. 8:11-13; 11:28, RSV, NIV; 11:31, RSV; 12:11).

Central to God's hostility towards the institution of the papacy was that it set aside the good news central to Scripture. And the good news is salvation by grace through faith in Jesus Christ alone. To deprive the people of God's atonement for sin through the death of His Son is surely a very serious offence.

Sad to say, Roman Catholic theologians continue to teach that Christ's sacrifice on Calvary was not sufficient to atone for sin, but has to be repeated again and again in 'the sacrifice of the mass'. They teach that the elements of the mass *in reality* become the body and blood of Christ. Between man and God the papacy interposes the priesthood; it denies man the privilege of confessing his sins to God. In place of Christ, our Mediator, it interposes the saints and the cult of the Blessed Virgin.

Though the New Testament could not be clearer that man's salvation is by grace through faith in Jesus Christ, the papacy asserts that man's salvation depends on his works – and that an ever-burning hell awaits him if he has not worked his passage to heaven.

Finally, they assert that 'tradition not scripture' 'is the rock on which the church of Jesus Christ is built' and that the Church can, therefore, in certain circumstances, set aside Bible-based truth and God-given commands.*

This is clearly the perversion of Christianity against which Daniel, Paul and John so specifically warned.

As I examine its beliefs, review its record and regard its pomp, I see the parallels of prophecy, thank God for His detailed warnings, and take my stand with the martyr who said, 'Christ is my Priest; His blood is my sacrifice; His altar is my confessional.'

There is at least one thing, however, that still may be worrying you.

The power and influence of the papacy did not end in 1798.

Prophecy does not say that it ended. Rather, that at the end of 1,260 years of supremacy it 'received a death-blow' (Rev. 13:3, NEB).

Is there a hidden menace in the next clause of the verse?

'But the mortal wound was healed. The whole world went after the beast in wondering admiration . . . .'

Are we to assume that the greatest days of 'the beast' are still to come?

---

* N. Nampom, SJ, *Catholic Doctrine as Defined by the Council of Trent*, pages 157, 543; H. J. Holtzmann, *Canon and Tradition*, page 263; *Catechism of the Council of Trent*, translated McHugh and Callan, pages 258, 259; H. Tuperville, *An Abridgement of the Christian Doctrine*, page 58; A. J. Grant, *History of Europe*, 1494-1610, page 267.

Incoming **storm**

Preacher Edward Irving and writer Thomas Carlyle were at a New Year's
Eve party. The party was at Annan, a town on the wild west coast of
Scotland. The house throbbed to the skirl of the bagpipes and the pounding
feet of the dancers. Suddenly Carlyle and Irving felt out of place. At ten
minutes to midnight they stepped out into a stormy night. Above the Solway
Firth they watched incoming storm clouds and heard the cannoning thunder.
Somewhere nearby, an angry, pounding sea was thrashing the harbour walls.
As the old year vanished before the new, Carlyle was caught up in the
enormity of it all. 'We stand at the centre of immensities, at the conflux of
eternities!' he exclaimed.

In terms of Bible prophecy, we see signs of an incoming storm. The
world's midnight is approaching.

Revelation 16:12-15 describes the coalition of three forces that will com-
bine against God's people in the final, decisive conflict before the return of
Jesus Christ:

'I saw three evil spirits that looked like frogs; they came out of the mouth
of the **dragon**, out of the mouth of the **beast** and out of the mouth of the
false prophet. They are spirits of demons performing miraculous signs,
and they go out to the kings of the whole world, to gather them for the battle on the great day of God Almighty. "Behold, I come like a thief! Blessed
is he who stays awake . . . ." '

The dragon, the beast and the false prophet: these are the thunderheads of
the incoming storm.

What do they represent?

✪ The **dragon** represents Satan himself, the evil angel who fought a war against God in heaven and, with one-third of the heavenly host, was expelled. Subsequently, he and his demon followers had been the enemies of God and His Church on earth. For most of earth-history the dragon had preferred to work through earthly powers. The significance of his presence in the final, end-time coalition is that Satan himself will have a hands-on role in the final conflict against God's people (Revelation 12).

✪ The **beast** we encountered in the last chapter. After 1,260 years of dominance, the beast-power received a 'fatal wound'. But this 'fatal wound' was 'healed'. And 'the whole world went after the beast in wondering admiration' (Rev. 13:3, NEB). Following the defeat of Napoleon, the papacy was among the first of the European powers to be reinstated. Its strength has grown steadily since then.

✪ The **false prophet** is identified with the second beast of Revelation 13, the first representing the papacy. The first beast had arisen out of the sea; symbolic of the fact that its base was in a populous part of the earth. The second beast (verse 11) came out of the earth; symbolic of the sparsely populated continent on which the pioneers founded the United States. The second beast resembled a lamb, but it spoke like a dragon and, when the chips were down, joined with the first beast in precipitating the life-or-death crisis for God's people. Modern scholars of Bible prophecy like Dwight Nelson, Clifford Goldstein and Marvin Moore identify the lamb-like beast of Revelation 13 and the false prophet of Revelation 16 with the USA – in the grip of intolerant forces.

✪ *Satan with a hands-on role.* ✪ *The beast more powerful than ever before.* ✪ *And the USA, once the refuge of the victims of intolerance in other countries, now itself a major instrument of intolerance.*

Scary, yes? But how could it come about?

It already *is* coming about.

The New Age movement

'Our fight is not against any physical enemy: it is against organizations and powers that are spiritual. We are up against the unseen power that controls this dark world, and spiritual agents from the very headquarters of evil.' Ephesians 6:11, 12, Phillips.

The devil's hands-on role is made possible by the New Age movement. This movement has many *faces* and *phases*. Its principal ingredients are astrology, Eastern religions (Buddhism and Hinduism) and the hard-core occult.

The New Age movement is based on the two primal lies used by Satan in Eden: 'You shall be as gods', and 'You shall not die'.

This bandwagon began to roll in the nineteenth century.

Weird knockings in the night had been heard in the Fox family home in Hydesville, New York State. The Fox family included John and Margaret and their daughters Margaretta and Kate. There was some story of a tinker who had met a violent death in the vicinity of their home.

On the night of 31 March 1848, Katie, 12, and Margaretta, 15, decided to get to grips with these mysterious knockings. Katie sat up in bed and flung out a challenge: 'Mr Splitfoot, do as I do.' And, in the hours that followed, the girls worked out a sort of Morse Code with the highly intelligent alien being. Of course, in identifying the alien as 'Mr Splitfoot' – the devil – young Katie had scored a psychic hole-in-one.

This is how modern spiritualism began. For Satan it was an impersonation game by which through the rigmarole of seances his demons could impersonate 'the spirits of the dead'. By posing as 'the beloved dead', demons could ensnare human beings at their most vulnerable: at the time of bereavement.

As spiritualism developed, a more sinister, though, at first, lower-profile movement had come into existence. It was founded by Madame Helena Blavatsky. Born in 1831 in Russia, Blavatsky became a circus performer, then spiritist medium, before settling in an Indian ashram and imbibing the ideas of the gurus: Eastern meditation techniques, reincarnation, channelling 'the spirits of the masters' (dead gurus).

By 1875 Blavatsky had migrated to the United States where she founded the Theosophical Society and began writing books which, she said, were dictated to her by the spirits.

Following Blavatsky's death the leadership of the movement fell first to British celebrity Annie Besant, then to Alice Bailey, and finally to Benjamin

Spiritist mediums claim to communicate with dead relatives. New Age channellers claim to communicate with long-dead gurus

Creme. While spiritualism claimed to communicate with dead relatives, the founders of the New Age movement claimed to 'channel' long-dead gurus and to be the repository of 'the wisdom of the ages'.

New Age ideas did not gain a mass following until the 1960s. The pied pipers of the sixties generation, the Beatles, spent their summers with Indian gurus and worked the esoteric messages of the gurus into their lyrics. By 1970 Indian gurus were flying West on one-way tickets – to become fabulously wealthy in the USA. Soon everyone was using the vocabulary of Hinduism and Buddhism. Yoga was widely practised and so were meditation techniques – to render the mind 'vacant possession'.

Will Baron describes his experience in the book *Deceived by the New Age*. Whatever 'face' of New Age attracted converts, the majority of them were drawn into hard-core occult activities such as channelling dead gurus, or 'masters' or 'christs'. Baron, in common with all major New Age figures, was a channeller. What this meant, in practice, was that after appropriate meditation techniques were followed, the mind and body of the channeller became possessed by an alien being, and an alien voice spoke through his or her mouth.

New Age leader Benjamin Creme coined the term New Age in 1977. He announced that 'the Age of Pisces' (Christianity) would soon be replaced by 'the Age of Aquarius' (New Age) in which a new world messiah would preside over a new world order. The radical materialism of the 1980s and 1990s massively increased the following of New Age. Materialism proved an inadequate diet for the human spirit and, because Christianity appeared to be in retreat, the new spirituality took on a pagan, New Age form.

New Age has had a major impact on Hollywood. All over the world there are specialist New Age shops full of books and crystals and assorted paraphernalia. In many general bookshops in the West, the Christian section has already been replaced by the New Age/Occult section. New Age has entered the classroom side by side with comparative religion. A disproportionate number of films on both big screen and small screen subscribe to the view that death is 'just a gateway to a new dimension'. And, too late, the popular theologians have realized that their doctrine of the immortality of the soul, drawn from paganism, has created the space for the *new* paganism.

Meanwhile, as time goes on, New Agers become more and more excited. Their 'New Age messiah', 'the Lord Maitreya', is about to declare himself. . . .

The revived papacy

At no time since the high Middle Ages has the papacy had more influence on world affairs than during the last two decades.

The signal for a resurgence of Vatican power was the election to the papal throne of John Paul II, the Polish Pope.

David Willey has published *God's Politician* (Faber and Faber). Willey, a long-time pope-watcher and sympathizer, having become disillusioned by the cynical manipulation of politicians by the Pope, decided to set his shocking story down for all to read. Atheist writer A. N. Wilson in the *London Review of Books* wrote that Willey had built up a 'formidable case' for John Paul as both a 'spiritual dictator' and as the centre of a global spider's web in which no government was independent of his influence.

While Willey was disgusted with the activities of 'God's politician', Malachi Martin in *The Keys of this Blood* (Touchstone) appeared thrilled at both the achievements and evident aims of the modern papacy. With *Time* magazine, Malachi Martin provided detailed evidence of the co-operation between the American presidency and the papacy in the destruction of Communism. Beyond the destruction of Communism, Martin was sure, John Paul II and his successors would fight – and win – 'the battle for faith'. Martin believed that already, in practice, the papacy was the most powerful political institution in the world; and that, as time went on, this fact would become more widely accepted. He saw the Pope's power base as partly, though by no means exclusively, within the European Union. However, Martin believed that the rejuvenated papacy would have a global role.

All eyes on America

We live in a one-super-power world – and the Pentagon has plans to keep it that way.

There are real dangers in a one-super-power world. Many groups in the United States are no longer committed to the ideals of the Founding Fathers

To the intense embarrassment of the US administration, the *New York Times*, international, on 8 March 1992, leaked a 46-page 'top secret' document. That document set out America's military priorities in the post-Cold War era. Priority One of those plans was clearly that the USA would *remain* the world's one super power!

The last two decades have witnessed the rise and rise of America's Religious Right. Presidents, regardless of their political priorities, have displayed increasing sensitivity to the clout of the slick RR pressure group – with its vast computer network – and have increasingly shown a tendency to exchange cherished constitutional freedoms for political advantage.

The separation of Church and State in the USA has become a political figment rather than a constitutional fact. In foreign policy close co-operation between the American presidency and the papacy is well documented.* The cryptic symbols of Revelation 13 project a scenario in which the two 'beasts' – representing the papacy and an intolerant USA – would work together to determine the global agenda. The casualties of this co-operation? Personal and religious freedom.

The concluding verses of Revelation 13 make chilling reading.

A single-issue conflict.

A choice between a true and a false Sabbath.

A life-and-death choice.

The exclusion from all economic activity of those who stand for God's Way (Revelation 13:11-18).

Three candidates, then, for world dictator – or a coalition of three forces. Which?

A devil-driven New Age messiah with occult powers.

A charismatic pope.

A Religious-Right-dominated US president.

Since 'the spirits of demons performing miraculous signs' are behind the scenes seeking to pull the strings, the question, 'Will it be a world dictator or a coalition of three evil powers?', is academic and pointless.

It is pointless, too, for another reason.

When the scene has been set, but before the death decree of God's people is implemented, God will intervene.

Jesus will return.

' "Behold, I come like a thief!" ' says the risen Christ. ' "Blessed is he who stays awake!" ' Revelation 16:15. The point of prophecy is, remember: Forewarned is forearmed. As the end-time scene falls into place, Paul's warning, 'Put on God's complete armour . . .' (Eph. 6:10, 11, Phillips), comes with greater urgency.

Now is not the time to lose ourselves in the cosy, careless crowd.

The party's over!

Outside, a midnight storm is blowing up. The cannoning thunder and crashing waves are already audible.

* Bryan Hehir, 'Papal Foreign Policy', *Foreign Policy* [Spring 1990]; *Time*, 24 February 1992.

Time's last syllable

'*Tomorrow and tomorrow and tomorrow creeps in this petty pace from day to day to the last syllable of recorded time. And all our yesterdays have lighted fools away to dusty death . . . .*'

This was the murderous Macbeth reflecting on the futility of the present and the bleakness of the future – without Christ.

Tomorrow, tomorrow and tomorrow.

Let's look at three tomorrows: the world's tomorrow, God's tomorrow and your tomorrow.

The world's tomorrow

In 1919 George Keough was sitting in the concourse of Grand Central Station and reading the *New York Times*. The point of the article was that there were some things that could *never* happen. Among the things that could *never* happen, read Keough, was a ban effective throughout the USA on the production, sale, importation and consumption of all forms of alcohol: Prohibition. It simply was *not* on the cards. An impossibility! Before Keough had finished reading the article, there was an announcement over the PA system. The announcer said, 'An amendment has just been passed by the requisite majority in the US Congress to ban the production, sale, importation and consumption of all forms of alcoholic beverage in every state of the Union.'

It couldn't happen. But it did.

There is one word that a professional historian never uses: 'inevitable'. In the onward march of events nothing, but nothing, is inevitable. No ideology, no nation, no institution is unshakeable.

Surely the last few decades have proved that.

Epochs, these days, last only moments. When *was* it that history went into overdrive?

Was it in the mid-eighties when Gorbachev rose to the top of the pile in the then Soviet Union? Certainly it was then that freedom sped through

Central and Eastern Europe. Ideologies and regimes collapsed in face of people power. Things that couldn't happen happened anyway. Even the cleverest of pundits had failed to predict them.

And then the forces Gorbachev had unleashed turned against him. Nationalism and freedom-fever caught on in the Baltic republics, in Georgia, Russia and the Ukraine – and the USSR dissolved and, with it, Communism.

Another thing that couldn't happen, but did, was the collapse of apartheid. With the release of Nelson Mandella, fast-paced change in South Africa brought about majority rule and the collapse of the old system in a way, and in a time-frame, that no one could have predicted.

Ferment in the Middle East. And George Bush announced a 'new world order'. Ever since the 'new world order' was announced, international tragedies have followed on the heels of one another. Mass starvation in Ethiopia and the Horn of Africa. The awful blood-letting, destruction, and human trauma that has taken place in the Balkans. Ferment among the Kurds.

Behind all this, scientists are talking on television: the earth is becoming uninhabitable. Has the warning become so familiar that we are beginning to ignore it?

There is talk of earth death – total toxic overload – when the planet becomes uninhabitable. Will there be eco-Armageddon?

Occult forces overspread the earth like a foul miasma. New Age symbolism, books, mega-buck films and television programmes come at us from all angles.

The world's future does not look rosy. With all the freedom euphoria – and evident disenchantment with new regimes – has anyone noticed that the world has now been destabilized? That there has been so much change in such a short time that literally *anything* could happen?

What determines the world's tomorrow? Does the destiny of the human race rest entirely in the hands of half a dozen men who pull the strings in the planet's major power blocs? Are we at the mercy of the first terrorist group or Islamic state to get its hands on nuclear weapons? Will it all end with an ecological 'vanishing point'? Will the rise of ultra-nationalism in Russia push us back to another cold war, more glacial than the first – and bring back the nightmare prospect of a terminal nuclear winter?

The world's tomorrow? Desperately uncertain.

God's tomorrow

So what, then, of God's tomorrow? What of the future with God Unlimited at the helm?

On the Mount of Olives, within days of His crucifixion, Jesus talked about God's tomorrow and the world's closing time. His sermon is recorded in three gospels (Matthew 24, Mark 13, Luke 21). There would, said Jesus, be signals to look out for to indicate the imminence of His return and of earth's closing time:

○ FALSE CHRISTS AND FALSE PROPHETS.

In the strange-goings-on end of the Christian spectrum, there is no shortage of false prophets. And, from time to time, a false christ.

The New Age has provided us with lots of false christs *and* false prophets.

○ WARS AND REVOLUTIONS.

Wars have been a built-in part of the history of the planet since Jesus made this prediction. The difference in the past century has been one of scale. Horrendous as recent wars have been, the tremendous overkill capacity of the super-powers – the real weapons of mass destruction – were not even used.

✪ NATURAL DISASTERS.

In today's world some 800 million are destitute, and millions die every day because they are too hungry to stay alive.

✪ INCREASED SUFFERING AND PERSECUTION.

The totalitarian regimes of our own century have produced more martyrdoms for Christ than in the rest of the history of the Christian Church put together.

✪ THE CHRISTIAN GOSPEL TO EVERY NATION.

Of the 230 nations on planet earth few, if any, have been untouched by Christian endeavour. There have been major triumphs in recent decades for Gospel, Bible-based Christianity in Africa, the nations of Central and South America and of the South Seas. From nations with repressive regimes there is evidence that the Gospel is being preached. . . .

The indicators of the end are all too apparent. They are on every television newscast.

The earth is not a ball spinning out of control in space. God *is* in control. He *is* at the helm. And with the escalating evil and violence, all is not lost. Jesus concluded His Olivet sermon with these words: ' "When all this begins to happen, stand upright and hold your heads high, because your liberation is near." ' Luke 21:25-28, NEB.

Soon, and very soon, the heavens will 'depart as a scroll'. Jesus will return to triumph over evil, to bring justice and judgement, to vindicate the character of God – and to build a new world.

The world's tomorrow? Desperately uncertain. God's tomorrow? Totally certain. The day of the Lord. The day He comes.

Your tomorrow

So what of *your* tomorrow?

Everything will depend upon your attitude towards Jesus Christ – today.

There are two appointments in the future that you and I must keep, neither of which we can put into our diaries: death and judgement; or the coming of Christ and judgement. That much is certain.

How we stand in the judgement will depend on whether or not we know the Judge. Jesus is both Judge and Saviour.

How should we relate to Jesus Christ today? We must accept His death in our place. His hands were pierced for the wrong things our hands have done. His feet were spiked for the wandering paths our feet have trod.

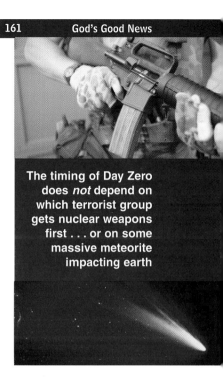

The timing of Day Zero does *not* depend on which terrorist group gets nuclear weapons first . . . or on some massive meteorite impacting earth

We cannot make ourselves 'worthy' or 'righteous'. But as we accept Christ's sacrifice on Calvary on our behalf then we are Christ's, and the second coming is the ultimate good news. For those who are 'in Christ Jesus' there need be no fear of condemnation (Rom. 8:1).

Finally, a word of encouragement. Then a word of warning.

However the world ends, it will *not* depend upon those who work the world's super-powers, or upon the eco-system or the whim of some half-mad dictator or terrorist. It will be the Day of the Lord. Our confidence on that day must be entirely on our personal relationship with Jesus Christ: the One who died for our sins, who has already conquered death, who is both Judge and Saviour – and who said, 'Let not your hearts be troubled . . . I will come again.' John 14:1-3, KJV.

A word of warning? Jesus said, 'Watch therefore, for you do not know the day when your Lord will come.' The question is, *Is* He your Lord? *Have* you accepted Him as your Saviour?

C. S. Lewis said, 'I wonder whether the people who ask God to interfere openly and directly in the world quite realize what it will be like when He does.'

When the Author walks on to the stage the play is over. It will be something so overwhelming that it will strike us either with irresistible love or irresistible terror. Then it will be too late to choose.

Today God in Christ stretches out His hand to give us forgiveness for the past, an abundant life for the present, and a glorious hope of an assured future. The decision as to whether we accept God's offer is made now.

The day **He comes**

On the day He comes it will be 'business as usual' – *He* said so!

On the day God draws a line across history and, for the sake of His faithful, says, 'Enough!' (Matt. 24:22) . . . on the day when Jesus returns to rescue His beleaguered people excluded from economic activity and facing a death decree (Rev. 13:17) . . . on the day, the date of which is God's secret and God's alone (Matt. 24:36) . . . on *that* day, what will be going on, on the surface of the planet that has reached Omega?

There will be an epidemic of fear, and a feeling of menace (Luke 21:26). Because the world has been held to ransom by some terrorist group with a nuclear facility? By occult forces running rampant because Satan knows that his last hours have come?

Perhaps.

Jesus said that, a prevailing atmosphere of fear notwithstanding, it will be 'business as usual' on earth on the day He comes. The pursuit of pleasure in its various forms will be going on uninterrupted. The institutions of commerce will be doing brisk business. The Information Super Highway will be absorbing the attention of many. The skylines of the cities will be broken by great cranes as man builds on the assumption that time will last for ever. Sensualists will be absorbed by sensual things. Materialists will be absorbed by material things. People will be pursuing their plans, oblivious to the fact that in God's eternal plan this is the Last Day, the day to make an end in order to make a beginning, the day He comes (Luke 17:25-31).

Except for God's faithful few, the scene in the sky on the day He comes will be a total surprise (1 Thess. 5:2, 4; 2 Peter 3:10; Rev. 3:3; 16:15).

Is there any chance of ignoring the close of history?

' "The day of the Son of Man will be like lightning flashing from one end of the sky to the other." ' Luke 17:24, Phillips.

It will be the most audible, and the most visual event since time began.

No one, not even the dead, will sleep through this one!

The first resurrection

'There will be the shout of command, the archangel's voice, the sound of God's trumpet, and the Lord himself will come down from heaven. Those who have died believing in Christ will rise to life first; then we who are living at that time will be gathered up along with them in the clouds to meet the Lord in the air. And so we will always be with the Lord.' 1 Thess. 4: 16, 17, GNB.

Part of that great rescue operation will be the resurrection of those who have died committed to Christ.

What a reunion! On the day He comes, those we have loved long since and lost a while will rise to eternal life. 'This same Jesus' (Acts 1:11) who ascended to heaven leaving behind bemused disciples; *this same Jesus* who touched the untouchable, loved the unlovable, who befriended the lonely and the ostracized; *this same Jesus* who lived, died and rose again that, subject to our own choice, we might receive His proffered gift of salvation (2 Cor. 5:21); *this same Jesus* – will raise the dead to life!

And, when they rise, though recognizable, they will be without the taint of that which brought them to the grave – disease, disaster, age. Their resurrection bodies will be like the resurrection body of their resurrected Lord (Phil. 3:21).

Great good news. The best! Families reunited! No more partings!

The beginning of an eternal adventure. . . .

The grapes of wrath

But the day He comes will not be good news for everyone.

'Then the kings of the earth, the princes, the generals, the rich, the mighty, and every slave and every free man hid in caves and among the rocks of the mountains. They called to the mountains and the rocks, "Fall on us and hide us from the face of him who sits on the throne and from the wrath of the Lamb! For the great day of their wrath has come, and who can stand?" ' Revelation 6:15-17, NIV.

On the day He comes it will be too late to make last-minute decisions. The day of grace will have passed. Even the richest and the mightiest will not find a last-minute exit door to some remote corner of outer space. They will be trapped on earth – praying for anything, *anything*, to hide them from the face of the rejected Saviour.

While the righteous of all ages – those alive at Jesus' coming and those who have been raised from death – exodus earth for Heaven to shouts of welcome from Jesus Himself, those living who have rejected His salvation will be thrown into a state of ultimate panic.

Those involved in Exodus Earth will be those with surrendered, cleansed, transformed lives – who have been to Calvary. Those who have accepted the great gift of salvation by grace through faith in Jesus Christ alone. But as they move through the glittering star-studded corridor of Orion, a living starship *en route* to the city of God, they will leave behind them on earth myriads who know they have made the wrong decision.

So far, in His dealings with men, God's wrath has been tempered with mercy. Not so now (Isa. 28:21; Rev. 14:10; 2 Peter 3:9).

The day of opportunity has been a long one. But now time is about to turn upon its hinge and become eternity; and wrongs must be righted, God's justice finally exacted. If God permitted rebellion to go unpunished for ever, men would be left to conclude that it makes little difference whether they obey God or not.

Jesus promised His disciples in all ages, 'I will come again and will *take you to myself.*' John 14:1-3, RSV. Paul wrote that at the first resurrection the saints of all ages will be 'caught up together' from the earth 'to meet the Lord in the air', and will 'always *be with the Lord*' (1 Thess. 4:17, RSV).

The righteous dead 'came to life', says John, in 'the first resurrection' and 'reigned *with Christ* a thousand years' – not on earth, but in heaven (Rev.

The day He comes will represent 'time's up' for the planet – no time for last-minute decisions

20:4, 5, RSV, italics in texts supplied). Having embarked upon their eternal reward, the saints have now received immortality as a gift.

How will they spend their thousand years in heaven 'with Christ'? Paul had told the Corinthians that 'the saints will judge the world'. In Revelation, John says that he 'saw thrones, and seated on them were those to whom judgement was committed' (Rev. 20:4; 1 Cor. 6:1-3; Matt. 19:28). It would appear that, during the thousand years, the redeemed participate with Christ and the angels in examining the life records of those who have adamantly resisted God's love and mercy.

Meanwhile, what will be happening on earth?

In Revelation 19 John describes the scene. Figuratively, we have a picture of Christ riding out from heaven on a white horse in His role as Commander of 'the armies of heaven' to deliver His people from their bloodthirsty foes who have 'gathered to make war against him who sits upon the horse and

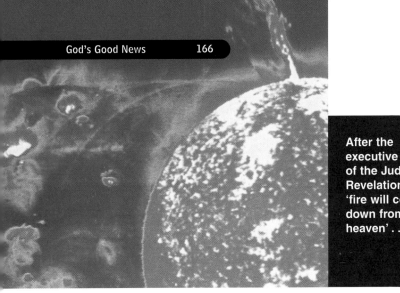

After the executive phase of the Judgement, Revelation says 'fire will come down from heaven'...

against his army'. (Rev. 19:13-15, 19, 21, RSV; compare 14:14-20).

Paul promised that those who had rejected God's salvation and had persecuted the saints would, on the day He comes, 'be destroyed with the breath of his mouth' (2 Thess. 2:8; 1:6-8, NRSV).

We have seen that John speaks of the resurrection of the saints at the coming of Jesus as 'the first resurrection'. Both Jesus and Paul spoke in terms of two resurrections; one for the just, one for the unjust (Luke 14:14; John 5:28, 29; Acts 24:15; Rev. 20:5).

Two resurrections, then. One for the righteous. One for the wicked.

The two resurrections will *not*, apparently, be simultaneous.

John declared, 'The rest of the dead', that is the wicked dead of all ages, 'did not come to life until the thousand years were ended' (Rev. 20:5-9). During the thousand years while the righteous are with Christ in heaven, the earth is one vast morgue. Satan is 'bound' to this planet 'for a thousand years . . . that he should deceive the nations no more, till the thousand years were ended. After that he must be loosed for a little while.' (Verses 2, 3, RSV.)

But, 'when the thousand years are ended, Satan will be loosed from his prison and will come out to deceive the nations' again. Hence, at the end of the thousand-year period, the second resurrection – that of the wicked – occurs. Satan is again surrounded by his own (Rev. 20:2, 3, 5, 7, 8, 13). Christ called this 'the resurrection of damnation' (John 5:28, 29, KJV).

The scene will be an awful one, beyond description. John expresses it this way: 'Their number is like the sand of the sea. And they marched up over the broad earth and surrounded the camp of the saints and the beloved city.' At the end of the thousand years, John also saw 'the holy city, new Jerusalem, coming down out of heaven from God' (Rev. 20:5-9; 21:2; compare Zech. 14:1-4, RSV).

In John's description, the New Jerusalem becomes the 'camp of the saints' (Rev. 20:9, RSV). From this we assume that, when it descends from heaven at the end of the thousand years, the saints descend in it.

The scene is a striking one.

Inside the city – Jesus and the saved of all ages.

Outside the city – Satan and the wicked of all ages.

Satan and his demon-driven hosts are determined on one last onslaught on God, His throne and His city.

This is the scene for the Final Judgement. Every being who has ever lived is present.

✪ In the Pre-Advent judgement in the heavenly sanctuary, Christ has declared that the saints have been saved by His death on Calvary.

✪ During the thousand years, the saints have the opportunity of reviewing the cases of the lost and establishing the justice of God.

✪ Now, the third and final stage of judgement takes place. The Executive Judgement. The wicked all stand before the throne (see Rev. 19 and 20). Books are opened. The Book of Life contains the list of those who are saved. Other 'books', the records of those who are unsaved. The cases of the saved are not reviewed at this time. But the wicked are now 'judged by what was written in the books, by what they had done' (Rev. 20. See also Phil. 4:3; Rev. 3:5; 13:8; 17:8; 21:27; 22:19; 20:11, 12, RSV).

Those who have spurned God's mercy stand speechless. No one has an excuse to offer. All acknowledge the justice of God (Rom. 14:11; Phil. 2: 10, 11).

There is a long moment of awful silence. Then there is the fateful sentence.

Immediately, says John, 'fire came down from heaven', and 'if anyone's name was not found written in the book of life, he was thrown into the lake of fire'. This John calls 'the second death', in contrast to the first death which is the natural lot of all men. The flames burn until they have done their work. There is *no* 'ever-burning hell fire' (Rev. 20:9, 14, 15, RSV).

All that is left is for the earth to be purged by fire of every last vestige of the reign of evil (2 Peter 3:10-13; Mal. 4:1).

Paradise restored

What is left of the great prophetic futurama to happen now?

Peter concluded his description of the purging of the earth of all evil with a note of glorious hope; 'According to his promise we wait for new heavens and a new earth in which righteousness dwells.'

A new heaven and a new earth will be created for God's people

2 Peter 3:10-13, RSV. In vision, the apostle John tells of seeing 'a new heaven and a new earth', after 'the first heaven and the first earth had passed away', and of hearing God's voice proclaim: ' "Behold, I make all things new." ' Revelation 21:1, 5.

'Then', John continues, 'I heard a great voice from the throne crying, "See! The home of God is with men, and he will live among them. They shall be his people, and God himself shall be with them, and will wipe away every tear from their eyes. Death shall be no more, and never again shall there be sorrow or crying or pain. For all those former things are past and gone." ' Revelation 21:2-4, Phillips.

God had given glimpses of this glorious new home on earth to His servants down through the centuries. Isaiah had described a time beyond time, and an earth unearthly, cleansed of the curse, when a little child would lead wild beasts, when the lion and the lamb would lie down together, when no one would hurt or destroy in all God's new creation and when, 'from sabbath to sabbath, all flesh shall come to worship before me, says the Lord' (Isa. 66:22, 23; 35:1, 2, 6; 65:17, NRSV).

Paul had told his converts in Corinth that the people who would inhabit the new earth would have real bodies, perfect and immortal. The saints would, he said, recognize their friends and see one another 'face to face' (1 Cor. 15:35-41; 13:12, RSV).

In this new earth there would not only be perpetual life, but perpetual health and vigour. The bloom of youth would remain on everyone's face for eternity. Pain and illness, death and destruction would be no more than distant memories, if that. No heart attacks. No malignant melanomas. No cerebral palsy. No muscular dystrophy. No multiple sclerosis. No rheumatism or arthritis. And no grim funeral processions – ever!

Paradise restored.

The inheritance of sinners saved by grace.

No more war, famine, atrocity, rape, AIDS, earthquakes, car crashes, rail crashes, plane crashes, violence in the streets, on the terraces, in the schools, in the home. All over. For ever.

Glorious good news from God! The time is coming when men and women of goodwill can live happily together under a universal government where there will be security, opportunity, prosperity and justice for all.

What an adventure! What an *eternal* adventure!

Do you plan to be in on that adventure?

It's a sobering thought that the decision as to whether we shall be inside or outside the city at the time of the final judgement, whether our names will be part of the Book of Life or of that other book – those decisions are taken now by us.

The risen Christ, through the Holy Spirit and the pen of John, concludes the canon of Scripture with an urgent word of warning, and with the most open invitation it is possible to extend.

' "See," ' says the risen Lord, ' "I am coming soon; . . . I am the Alpha and the Omega, the first and the last, the beginning and the end." ' Revelation 22:12, NRSV.

How will it be with you on the day He comes?

Do you know the Saviour?

Have you accepted Him as your own?

On the day He comes, will you meet your Lord as your greatest Friend?

The end;
a new beginning

The world's tomorrow is bleak.

God's tomorrow is certain. Jesus will return to establish a perfect kingdom.

Your tomorrow depends on what you choose today. There is God's Way that leads to life everlasting. There is man's way – neon-lit by Satan to entice the unwary – that leads to emptiness, purposelessness and, ultimately, oblivion.

God's offer of salvation is open to all.

We begin by approaching Him in prayer to say: 'Lord, I want to start afresh. I have looked at Your salvation and know that I can never deserve it. I come to You just as I am, pleading for forgiveness of my sins and accepting Jesus as my personal Saviour. Only through His death, resurrection and righteousness can I be saved. At Calvary I see Your limitless love and goodness; and I see the awfulness of my sins. Lord, through Your Holy Spirit, come dwell within me and expel all that is awful; take over my life and make it new. Amen.'

Jesus said that the first essential for those who would enter His kingdom is: 'You *must* be born again.'

'Born again' implies a complete revolution in your life.

As you live your new life in company with the risen Christ, and through the power of His Spirit, there will be struggles and failures. Even the great apostle Paul knew that though he wanted what was best he often disappointed God. Once he cried out, 'O wretched man that I am! Who will deliver me?' Then he answered his own question, as you must answer it when you feel the way he felt: 'Through Jesus Christ our Lord.' Paul continued with the ultimate reassurance for the Christian: 'There is therefore now no condemnation to those who are in Christ Jesus.' Romans 7:14-8:1, NKJV.

The more you look at your sin, the more sinful you will become. Look to the Saviour, and you will be changed into His likeness.

The way to peace

Christianity is built on one foundation. What is it? That, in Jesus Christ, God invaded human history – to die in man's place, to rest in man's tomb, to destroy for ever, on man's behalf, the thrall of death.

The death, the burial and the resurrection of a Man, a God-man, the Lord Jesus Christ: these three acts make Christianity different from every other faith.

Nothing is more important in all of our lives than that we grasp the full significance of these acts. That is why Jesus arranged that, at the very outset of the Christian life, man should take part in a symbolic ceremony to enforce upon his mind these three acts and their meaning: cleansing and death to an old life, the burial of that old life for ever, resurrection to a new life – which has no end. The symbolic ceremony is called baptism.

'Don't you know that all of us who were baptized into Christ Jesus were baptized into his death? We were therefore buried with him through baptism into death in order that, just as Christ was raised from the dead through the glory of the Father, we too may live a new life. If we have been united with him in his death, we will certainly also be united with him in his resurrection.' Romans 6:3-5.

The lowest spot on earth

Jericho is the oldest city in the world, and is built on the lowest spot on earth. Nearby is the weirdest, wildest expanse of barren, lunar-like mountains and valleys on the planet: the Wilderness of Judaea. Here John the

I need forgiveness

We must acknowledge our sins and our need of forgiveness when we come to Jesus. That's where new life begins

Baptist preached of the coming Messiah.

Men and women came out from Jerusalem, from Jericho, and even came south from the populous settlements around Galilee to listen to him. John called them to repent and, when they repented, he baptized them in the Jordan river.

Repentance means 'a change of mind'. The mountains and hills of pride and self-will are levelled. Crooked ways are straightened. Rugged places are smoothed – that we may receive Jesus.

To repent is to sense that material things are hollow; to look for light and life, while turning away from darkness and death.

Habits may rebel. Peace and joy may yet be far away. But the will has made its secret decision. Satan has been abandoned in favour of God.

In repentance we repent of our own sins. We acknowledge that we are at the end of our tether; there is nothing we can do for ourselves.

What are the symptoms of repentance?

First, *confession*. The 'OK-on-the-outside' man confessed that under the whitewash of his religious observances there was a mass of filth. The un-believer confessed that his refusal of faith was largely due to the fears he had of the high standards God would require of him. The masses confessed their selfishness and sensuality.

They confessed to God, and to one another. Right there on Jordan's bank feuds were reconciled; words of apology and forgiveness exchanged; hands grasped hands after years of alienation.

The second symptom of repentance was *results*. Peter speaks of *repentance* as a gift (Acts 5:31). Paul assures us that *faith* is a gift (Eph. 2:8). James and John the Baptist insist that after we have received these gifts there must be results. Our lives must bear evidence that they are aimed towards heaven (James 2:14-18; Matt. 3:8).

John did not believe that there was anything holy about the muddy waters of the Jordan. Baptism was a symbol. It meant death and burial as far as the past was concerned; and resurrection to a new and better future.

But John repeatedly gazed over the heads of the crowds, knowing that one day Someone would emerge by comparison with whom he was unworthy, a forerunner.

One day Jesus came down from Galilee. He asked John to baptize Him. John replied, ' "I need to be baptized by you, and do you come to me?" '

Note the reply of Jesus: ' "Let it be so now; it is proper for us to do this to fulfil all righteousness." ' Matthew 3:13-15.

John's faraway gaze fixed on Jesus. Though he had never quailed before monarchs, he shrank from Jesus. These publicans and sinners, these soldiers and common people – had every need to repent, confess, and be forgiven. In Jesus he saw One who was 'holy, harmless, undefiled'.

But Jesus told him, in effect, 'Anyone who wants to follow me all the way must follow me into the waters of baptism.'

So John baptized Jesus.

Why was Jesus baptized? 'To fulfil all righteousness.' For man to live as God would have him live, he must be baptized. By this act Christ sliced a trail of escape through the jungle of sin, leaving an example that none could misunderstand.

When we decide to follow in the footsteps of Jesus, those footsteps lead inevitably into the waters of baptism. By being baptized, *He* identified with our sins. By being baptized, *we* identify with His righteousness.

Baptism

Why do so many fail to follow the footsteps of Jesus into baptism? Do they confuse baptism with what has come to be known as 'christening'? Have they so far lost sight of what is symbolized by baptism that they are confused over the mechanics?

Those who understand Greek have no problem over the mechanics. The Greek word behind the word baptize is *baptizo*, literally 'to immerse under water, to immerse completely'.

**Baptism by immersion symbolizes the death,
burial and resurrection of Jesus**

John baptized 'in the River Jordan' (Mark 1:4, 5). ' . . . because there was plenty of water' (John 3:23). After His baptism, Jesus came 'up *out* of the water' (Mark 1:8-11, italics supplied).

'Have you forgotten that all of us who were baptized into Jesus Christ were, by that very action, sharing in his death? We were dead and buried with him in baptism, so that just as he was raised from the dead by that splendid revelation of the Father's power so we too might rise to life on a new plane altogether.' Romans 6:3, 4, Phillips.

Only baptism by immersion could symbolize death, burial and resurrection. Jesus told His disciples to go and teach and baptize all nations (Matt. 28:19, 20). And the record shows that they did (Acts 8:26-39; 16:30-34; 8:12).

Only baptism by immersion can symbolize the three central acts of Christianity: the death, burial and resurrection of Jesus – and what they mean for the sinner.

Time to decide

Jonathan Edwards wrote: 'When I look into my heart and take a look at its wickedness, it seems like an abyss infinitely deeper than hell.'

The great Christian, Augustus Toplady, wrote in his diary: 'My short-comings, my misdoings, my unbelief and my lack of love sink me to the lowest hell.'

The difference was that Toplady could add, 'were it not for Jesus my Righteousness and my Redeemer.'

Are you as conscious of the evil within you as these men were?

Man is more devil than angel, according to Scripture. Therefore he requires more than a change of environment; more than education, psychology or political idealism can offer him. He needs more than the outward trappings of religion. He needs cleansing and, through cleansing, death to an old life and resurrection to a new. He needs what Toplady had: 'Jesus my Righteousness and my Redeemer.'

Jesus said, 'Except a man be born of water and of the Spirit, he cannot enter into the kingdom of God.' John 3:5, KJV. Then He personalized it: ' "*You* must be born again." ' John 3:7, NKJV, italics suppied. There are no ifs and buts. This is the foremost imperative.

Jesus is saying that He will not take to heaven anybody who does not already have heaven in himself.

Each one of us is like a person who has fallen from the top of a sky-scraper – bound to meet with destruction unless some power going in the other direction takes hold of him.

Thank God that power is in Christ – His death, His burial, His resurrection.

We need power from without to cleanse us.

We need power from without to give us life.

We are dependent upon Another, even One who has slept the sleep of death and whose hands were pierced for the wrong things our hands have done, whose feet were spiked for the wrong paths our feet have trod, whose brow was thorn-crushed because of the wrong thoughts our minds have har-boured, whose heart was broken because of the wrong things our hearts have loved, whose side was riven to convince us – sinners – that the way to

God's heart is wide open.

Anyone, any place, any time, who comes to Him is always, always, always accepted.

Nothing, but nothing, can take the place of the cleansing that God has provided through Christ.

Inner peace is found through the three acts which make Christianity different from any other religion – the three acts symbolized by baptism.

Inner peace is found only in Jesus Christ.

Over to you.

There are no more words to be said.

You need silence, and you need prayer.

You have a decision to make.

As you make that decision
shut out from your
mind every scene
but Calvary,
every voice
but His
voice.